Rebecca Lenkiewicz

PLAYS ONE

Rebecca Lenkiewicz's *The Night Season* (National Theatre, 2004) received the Critics' Circle's Most Promising Playwright Award and was nominated for the Charles Wintour Evening Standard Award and the Susan Smith Blackburn Award. *Her Naked Skin* was the first play by a living female playwright to be staged on the Olivier stage of the National Theatre in 2008. Her other plays include *Soho – a Tale of Table Dancers* (Arcola Theatre, 2001), *The Painter* (Arcola), *The Typist* (Riverside Studios), *The Lioness* (Tricycle), *That Almost Unnameable Lust*, *Shoreditch Madonna*, *Blue Moon over Poplar* (Soho Theatre), *A Soldier's Tale* (Old Vic), *Invisible Mountains* (National Theatre), *Faeries* (Royal Opera House), *Justitia* (Peacock Theatre) and adaptations of Ibsen's *Ghosts* and *An Enemy of the People*.

REBECCA LENKIEWICZ

Plays One

The Night Season
Shoreditch Madonna
Her Naked Skin
The Painter

with an introduction
by the author

faber and faber

First published in 2013
by Faber and Faber Limited
74–77 Great Russell Street
London WC1B 3DA

This collection © Rebecca Lenkiewicz, 2013

The Night Season
first published by Faber and Faber Limited in 2004
© Rebecca Lenkiewicz, 2004
Shoreditch Madonna
first published by Faber and Faber Limited in 2005
© Rebecca Lenkiewicz, 2005
Her Naked Skin
first published by Faber and Faber Limited in 2008
© Rebecca Lenkiewicz, 2008
The Painter
first published by Faber and Faber Limited in 2011
© Rebecca Lenkiewicz, 2011

Typeset by Country Setting, Kingsdown, Kent CT14 8ES
Printed in England by CPI Group (UK) Ltd, Croydon CR0 4YY

A CIP record for this book
is available from the British Library

ISBN 978-0-571-30291-8

2 4 6 8 10 9 7 5 3 1

Contents

Introduction

Last night I went to my local pub, The Tiger. It was a Karaoke night. It's a large shabby room but the laser lights give it a David Lynch feel. The crowd is sparse, about twenty people. One old man wears a Russian hat and sings directly to his wife – 'These boots were made for walking'. She in turn gets up and directs her song to him – 'Ruby Tuesday'. The lyrics are much more naked sung by civilians. You truly hear what the song is about. The couple who run it have been doing it for many years. Carrying the equipment from pub to pub. Duets. Curiously the woman does not sing any more. I get up and stumble through 'Brand New Key' but I enjoy the adrenalin of those two minutes of words, instrumental, words, panic. My boyfriend Gary's Coldplay song is not on the system, his slip is torn up. He sings instead 'The Long and Winding Road'. I watch him and cry, partly vodka, partly the song, partly the day, but also just the fact of people and what they want and how they struggle. And the human voice. This is very much who we are, how we are. It's both beautiful and difficult.

Writing *The Night Season* was a cathartic experience. I was heartbroken and temping at the BBC. I had an inane postal job there. Manilla envelopes and power-crazy magazine editors. On Fridays a tea trolley would be wheeled round. There were whoops as people considered the treats. I wanted to run down the concrete fire stairs, anywhere, just away. I had finished an unfortunate acting job which led a troupe of us to Greece to perform at Epidaurus. I would mud and mask up with the rest of the chorus. Our wild women costumes were cut so high that our buttocks were on show. I felt far more like a Flintstone than a Bacchante. Epidaurus, we were informed, was the epicentre and root of all healing. Most of the girls were in tears most of the days. On my return writing was a pure escape. It took me higher than the internal repetitive bile I was experiencing. It was another self, my better half. The independence was intoxicating. Fevered nights ensued with me, myself and I. I was having a party in my head. Fun. A fictitious Irish family had partly sprung from my own but they were fast becoming fiercely independent. When the play was produced my tears were when I saw the actors warming up. Something about the happening of it there and then, we were all alive and together, the community and optimism of that moment. We'd gathered to tell a tale of nobodies from nowhere to strangers from anywhere and that touched me.

Shoreditch Madonna was a strange creature that came out of the dark. Writing it was more conscious. It was a commission so there was a venue for it besides the inside of my head. A diehard artist negotiates life in the shadows after being expelled from the bright lights. Who is in? Who is out? Who merely has to pixellate to gain plaudits? Real versus slick. It's about love and the desire to connect.

Her Naked Skin was the first play where I felt honour bound to do very real justice to the subject. It wasn't just a product of my meanderings. These were women who had lived and who had fought so bravely for the vote. Although all the characters are composites, I wanted to convey their incredible spirit and courage. It was a generation so different from ours in terms of values and decency. I wanted to make it present and not sepia. For these suffragettes to be extreme and brilliant but still part of their Edwardian world. I had read Mitch Mackenzie's book, *Shoulder to Shoulder*, a brilliant study which included harrowing firsthand accounts of the torture the women had endured in Holloway Prison. The force feeding, the humiliations. I had no idea of the sheer brutality before reading their testimonies. I wanted to alert a modern audience to the horrors they had been subjected to and survived.

The Painter was commissioned by the Arcola. In 2000 Mehmet Ergen had produced my first play *Soho* to open their new theatre. The building at that time was raw. Rubble. Concrete. Arctic. It was an old sweatshop. It was also huge. A rarity in fringe theatre. Mehmet and Leyla Nazli transformed it into a buzzing vibrant space. Initially we played to a group of five or six people sometimes harangued into coming to see it from the Turkish supermarket next door. But by the end of the run we were sold out and it felt like the birth of an important new theatre. It became a magical place. Ten years later they had to move. Mehmet asked me to write a play about an old paint works, their new building. I helped on one of the clearing days. It had been an African club but closed for decades. I swept pigeon skeletons out from the window sills. We both thought that Turner would be a wonderful subject for a play. Billy Turner inhabited my head. Sometimes when I felt in a rut I would take a walk around Victoria Park and just look upwards at the clouds. Turner changed my way of watching the formations. He would walk for miles. And sit on a hill for hours waiting for the right sky to happen. When it did he would say 'There it is' and start to sketch. I loved his difference from the usual society of painters. His direct approach to dealers who intimidated most painters. 'Ain't it worth more?' he'd ask.

So plays keep being written, strange love letters to the world. And one still waits for The Idea. The perfect idea. The perfect character. It is a semi-lunatic activity of hanging around for voices in one's head. Hoping that a distant relative of Myshkin or Raskolnikov or Masha or Winnie might visit. Shaw's St Joan resonated for me when I was at school, her beautiful speech when she tears up her confession because she realises she will be imprisoned. Lear's words to Cordelia as they are about to be locked up will always move me. I don't have a religion but if I have a faith it would be about achieving some sort of freedom. Somehow. Somewhere. One waits for the most perfect cloud formation.

Rebecca Lenkiewicz
December 2012

I've had a fascinating time in the production of these plays. I am deeply grateful to all those who have brought them to life. I am also indebted to Dinah Wood, my editor at Faber, for her brilliant support and intelligence.

THE NIGHT SEASON

For my family

The Night Season was first performed in the Cottesloe auditorium of the National Theatre, London, on 23 July 2004. The cast was as follows:

Lily O'Hanlon Annette Crosbie
Maud Kennedy Sarah-Jane Drummey
Rose Kennedy Justine Mitchell
Judith Kennedy Susan Lynch
Patrick Kennedy David Bradley
John Eastman John Light
Gary Malone Lloyd Hutchinson

Director Lucy Bailey
Designer Dick Bird
Lighting Designer Neil Austin
Music Roddy Skeaping
Sound Designer Neil Alexander
Dialect Coach Majella Hurley
Movement Caroline Pope
Assistant Director Virginia Elgar

Characters

John Eastman
in his thirties

Patrick Kennedy
in his fifties

Judith Kennnedy
in her thirties

Rose Kennedy
in her twenties

Maud Kennedy
in her twenties

Lily O'Hanlon
in her seventies

Gary Malone
in his thirties

Patrick is father to Judith, Rose and Maud.
Lily is their maternal grandmother.

The action takes place in and around
the Kennedys' home near Sligo.

Act One

SCENE ONE

The kitchen. Late. Lily sits playing patience by lamplight. 'Just the Way You Look Tonight' is playing quietly on the record player. Lily is variously singing to it and reciting psalms to herself. She sings and hums the song on and off during the next scene.

Judith's room. There are two beds. Maud and Judith are in one, while Rose sits on the other near the window.

Rose She never goes to bed now.

Maud Will you miss her when she dies?

Rose No.

Maud I hope she dies in her sleep, though. Peaceful.

Rose What did the doctor say? (*She lights up a cigarette.*)

Judith A few months. I thought you'd given up.

Rose I have.

Judith Right. 'Night.

Rose 'Night.

Patrick's room, next to Judith's. Both have a window. Patrick is asleep in bed. He is having a nightmare.

Patrick You . . . You'll get blood on the carpet . . . Who took the carpet? . . . Just leave me my tongue . . . I have uses for that. (*He groans as though he is being stabbed.*)

Judith's room. Maud opens the window.

Maud He's having a nightmare.

Rose He is a fucking nightmare.

Patrick's room.

Patrick (*asleep*) Sit still . . . It won't hurt . . . I have to cut your hair. (*He bellows.*)

The kitchen. Lily has heard Patrick's groan.

Lily Esther? Esther? What's he doing to you? Esther?

Judith's room.

Judith She never stops talking about Mum now.

Maud Did you ring Mum today?

Judith I left her another message.

Maud Why doesn't she come back, then?

Rose She's not interested.

Judith We should get Lily over to London.

Maud She'd never get on a plane.

Judith What if Lily dies without seeing her?

Rose She won't. Go and see Mum if you want to. You don't need an excuse.

Judith Do you not want to see her?

Rose No. I don't like her . . . What? I didn't choose not to like her. This fella's not turning up now, is he? I'm going back to my room.

Judith You can't. His flight might be delayed. Anything could've happened.

Rose Why doesn't he stay with the others at the hotel?

Judith He wanted to stay somewhere real.

Rose Christ . . . somewhere real?

Maud Do you think this fella will look like Yeats?

Judith He'll have to, won't he? You have to be similar. Like Kirk Douglas as Van Gogh.

Rose Or Charlton Heston as Moses.

Maud Maybe one of us'll fall in love with him.

Judith Goodnight.

Maud No . . . I couldn't do that to Kevin.

Rose Kevin's a communist. He'd understand.

Maud Mm. We've not had sex in ages. He says it's world issues are crushing his masculinity.

Rose How long is ages?

Maud Two months. Don't say anything, will you? . . . I've never seen him fully naked, you know.

Rose What do you mean?

Maud He doesn't like me to see his body. He's always got a long shirt on or something.

Rose But when you have sex?

Maud It's always in the dark. It feels fine. He just won't let me see it. Should it worry me?

Judith No. 'Night.

Maud 'Night.

Rose No. Some people have sex through a hole in the sheet, don't they?

Maud Is that supposed to make me feel better?

Rose I just mean by their standards Kevin's very liberal, isn't he?

9

Maud I suppose.

Rose Plus his mother's a freak. She's the type would have breastfed him till he was seven. Maybe he's a woman. Maybe it's all strapped on.

Maud No. He's just shy.

Judith Where did you leave Lily's diet sheet?

Rose Oh . . .

Judith You filled it in, didn't you? I've got to give it to the doctor tomorrow.

Rose I'll do it before you go.

Judith Rose. You said you'd do it.

Rose So I forgot. So report me to Amnesiacs Anonymous. I'll do it in the morning.

Judith It's meant to be done at the time.

Rose I remember what she ate.

Judith You should write things down, Rose. Make a list of important things you've got to do.

Rose If there was ever anything important to do, I would.

Rose smokes while Judith and Maud go to sleep. Lily sings the sailor song from Korda's Thief of Baghdad *and Rose echoes it to her just as the song is echoed in the film.*

Patrick's bedroom. Patrick wakes from sleep. He is drunk. He leans out of his window.

Patrick Is that the singing fucking sailor?

Rose stops singing, Lily keeps singing quietly.

Rose Yeah.

Patrick Does Sinbad happen to have a cigarette on her?

Rose Yeah.

Rose puts two cigarettes in her mouth, lights them both and gives one to Patrick.

Patrick That actor fella never came.

Rose No.

Patrick They said he'd be here Tuesday. I stayed in for him all day yesterday and today.

Rose But you never go out.

Patrick I stayed in.

Rose You've been asleep all day.

Patrick Yes. Staying in for him.

Rose Were you at the Pegasus tonight?

Patrick Tonight. Last night. Tomorrow night.

Rose Many people there?

Patrick Too many people. Do they have no homes to go to?

Rose Nikki behind the bar?

Patrick She was. Stood there under that blue light. The patron saint of the pissed. She haunts me. Those eyes, that dress, those breasts.

Rose Were the film people there?

Patrick Fucking circus. Gifford was showing off to the make-up girls. Doing the same old fucking light-bulb trick.

Rose Which one?

Patrick Smashing it in one hand while he drinks his pint with the other. I held the stool for Nikki while she changed the bulb. She had her jeans on tonight.

Rose 'Night, Dad.

Patrick That moon is fucking bright.

Rose Sweet dreams.

Patrick The devil takes care of his own.

They go to their beds.

SCENE TWO

The Pegasus. John Eastman sits down with a pint and a whiskey. He is very abstracted and quite drunk. He is wearing a dinner suit. Gary has also had a few drinks and approaches him.

Gary (*gives John a wallet, a script and a packet of cigarettes*) You left your stuff on the bar.

John Thanks.

Gary Are you all right?

John Yes. Thank you.

Gary Are you here with the film?

John Yes. You?

Gary No. I live here. Gary Malone.

John John.

Gary Are you an actor?

John Yes.

Gary Cigarette?

Gary offers John a cigarette. John tries to light it, but has difficulty because his hand is shaking. Gary lights his own and helps John to light his.

John Thanks. Can you help me, Gary? Later I need to get to this house. There's no phone number. Do you know where it is? Or where I can get a cab? (*He gives Gary his diary with the address written in it.*)

Gary No need . . . It's not far. I'll walk you there when you've finished your drink.

John I just need to know how to get there.

Gary Do you know the family?

John No. You do?

Gary Yeah, I do.

John What are you drinking?

Gary I've one at the bar (*to the barmaid*) I'm coming back for that, Nikki! (*to John*) Is that clothes she's wearing or underwear? (*to Nikki*) Get your thieving hands off that! You tell me when you want to go up to the cottage. No hurry.

John Did you ever do something irreparable, Gary?

Gary What?

John Something shameful you could never repair?

Gary sits down.

Gary You can't tell, can you?

John Why not?

Gary You might fix things later.

John Sometimes you know.

Gary What did you do? Did you kill someone?

John Do you think you know when you love someone?

Gary Yes. I think it's pretty clear.

John And if you do, you can do anything, can't you? Love makes you brave.

Gary It can work the other way. Make you an awful coward.

John No. Not real love. It makes you fearless. That's why people crave it. They want to be transformed.

Gary Maybe. You left someone behind?

John Yes. I should have picked her up in my arms and I didn't.

Gary Talk to her.

John It's too late.

Gary I'm sorry.

John Thanks . . . Your face changed.

Gary My face?

John When I showed you that address. Your expression changed.

Gary They do change, don't they? Else it'd be pretty fucking boring wouldn't it?

John 'But one man loved the pilgrim soul in you and loved the sorrows of your changing face.'

Gary You been learning Yeats?

John There's a lot in the script.

Gary He's got some great chat-up lines.

John Something happened to you in that cottage.

14

Gary Not something. Someone.

John And you love her?

Gary She . . . affects me.

John And she doesn't want you?

Gary I haven't asked lately.

John Were you together?

Gary We were. A long time ago.

John And now you're apart.

Gary I'm here. She's there.

John And she didn't fight for you?

Gary No, she didn't.

John That's pretty conclusive, isn't it?

Gary I'm going to get my drink. I'll walk you there when you're through.

Gary goes to the bar. John drinks his whiskey.

SCENE THREE

The kitchen. Late. Lily is in her chair. Rose enters and sits by the fire.

Lily Esther?

Rose No, it's me. Do you want a cigarette?

Lily Absolutely. Is the rain keeping you awake?

Rose lights two cigarettes and gives one to Lily.

Rose No.

15

Lily Esther used to come down like that. As a child. In the middle of the night. There's a man outside sat waiting by the wall in the rain. He has no shoes.

Rose (*goes to the window*) No. There's no one there. Do you want a drink?

Lily Yes. Why were you crying last night?

Rose gets them both a drink.

Rose I just felt blue. Thinking that things might never happen.

Lily Young men?

Rose No.

Lily You were scared you'd be a spinster all your life.

Rose I'm not a spinster. I'm single.

Lily Is that different?

Rose Very different.

Lily But neither of them has a man. You were crying because you're a spinster.

Rose Do you want to go to London with Judith and see Esther?

Lily No. There's too many directions there.

Rose I'm going to bed. Do you want anything?

Lily A lover.

Rose exits. Lily stares into the fire.

Do you see the lion in the fire, Esther? Do you remember your huge lion? We'd visit him in the shop and talk to him. Then one day he disappeared and you mourned him. But he was next to your bed in the dark, waiting . . .

A gentle knock on the door. Lily goes to it and opens it to John, who is barefoot and drunk. He is holding his muddy shoes.

John Hello. I'm John. The light was still on.

Lily You have no shoes.

John No. I took them off.

Lily You're wet. I'm Lily.

John I'm staying next door. In your cottage. Do you stay up all night, Lily?

Lily I don't like to be horizontal. Whiskey?

John I'd love one.

Lily I saw you. Waiting. Like the song. (*She sings a couple of lines from 'Lili Marlene'.*) People said I was like her because of my name and my face.

John Who were you like?

Lily Lili Marlene. He was tired marching and he thought of her and his bags got lighter. Would you like to dance?

John Dance?

Lily With me.

John I would, but . . .

Lily You don't want to. I see that.

John No. I'd love to. Shall we?

He takes her hand and gently dances cheek-to-cheek with her. They hold each other tighter. Marlene Dietrich's 'Lili Marlene' plays.

Lily Do you hear the music?

John No. But I can imagine it.

Lily Do you dance with everyone?

John No. I don't.

Lily Nobody's paying you, are they? To dance with me?

John No, they're not.

Lily Nobody's behind that red curtain, are they?
Watching? Laughing?

John No. Nobody's there.

Lily Your feet are naked. They're deeply personal. I
don't remember the last time I was alone with a man. I
don't remember what a man is like. I knew men in a past
life. You're real, though, aren't you?

John I think so, Lily. I don't really know.

Lily There's too many details for it not to be happening.
Our shadows are dancing together too. Authentic.
You've a wonderful touch. I feel so beautiful I could die.
John, would you stay with me tonight? Please. I'll clean
your shoes for you in the morning.

John Course I'll stay with you. And I'll clean my own
shoes.

> *They dance. Lily sits down on the floor. John puts a
> blanket over her and lies down to sleep. Lily sits and
> watches him. The music fades.*
>
> *Outside. Gary is standing in the rain, very drunk. He
> is looking up at Judith's window.*

Gary Judith? Do you want to come out for a walk?
Judith . . . I played chess the other night against myself
and each of the pieces looked like you. Even the bishops.
I sit in my room and I wait for you. Thinking you might
turn up on the doorstep in the rain. I'd make you tea
and dry your hair. Fuck it. People ring the bell and it's

not you. I'm going away. 'I have loved a queen beyond measure and exceeding long' . . . and now I'm tired. So fucking tired. And I'm going away.

SCENE FOUR

Morning. Lily is still watching John.

Lily You look like a child.

John (*waking*) Morning.

Lily Good morning, John. How are you?

John I'm fine. Bit of a headache.

Lily You fell off cliffs in the night and shouted. (*She puts a feather in his hair.*)

John Did I keep you awake?

Lily No. I don't sleep. Would you like some music? I've a surprise record for you, John. Can you guess what it is?

Judith's room. Judith, Rose and Maud are getting dressed and making their beds.

Rose Are these my tights? I can't live like this for six weeks. Like a fucking gypsy.

Maud How much'll we get, do you think?

Rose Nothing if Dad gets it first.

Judith Don't let Kevin get his hands on it either.

Maud What do you mean?

Judith Don't let him beg it off you.

Maud He wouldn't. He's not like that.

Rose He asks you for his bus fare home.

Maud He only asked me for it once.

Judith Twice. And he asked me to delete his library fines.

Maud Which you didn't do. Which I ended up paying.

Judith Which I gave back to you. He was arrogant. He said the silence signs were forms of government censorship. Plus I see him nicking books.

Maud It's not a crime to lend him money, is it?

Judith Does he give it back to you?

Maud He means to.

Judith I'm not attacking you. I'm just saying that when Dad gives you that money –

Rose If Dad gives you that money –

Judith Go and buy yourself something nice. Don't give it to your man.

Rose Do you think Kevin's actually terrified by his own genitalia?

Maud I don't know why I ever tell you things.

Judith I'm late. Will you two get Lily breakfast?

Rose No. We'll ritually starve her and record her reactions in her diet journal.

Judith, Rose and Maud exit the bedroom.

The kitchen. Lily and John are sitting up on the floor with a blanket over them. They have tea, toast and cigarettes. Marlene Dietrich's 'Johnny' is playing.

Lily Shall we listen to it again?

John Three times was fine, thank you. Just perfect.

Lily Would you like some more tea? Toast? Cigarettes? Whiskey? Cheese? Eggs? Tea? Toast? Jam?

John Nothing. Thanks.

Judith, Rose and Maud enter.

Judith Lily . . .

Lily Yes . . . This is Judith, Rose and Maud. This is John.

John Morning.

Judith You're John Eastman?

John I am. I got here very late last night.

Lily John's a wonderful dancer.

Judith Good. John . . .

John Lily asked me to stay in here with her, so I did.

Judith Right. Are you all right, Lily?

Lily I'm fine, Judith. How are you?

Judith I'm well. Very well. I have to go to work. Shall I show you next door?

Maud I'll take him.

Judith I'll see you, then.

John Bye.

Judith Should I call Dad before I go?

Patrick enters with just a long shirt on.

Patrick I don't know why you have to play music in the morning, Lily. And why do you play the same fucking song over and over? You're not a fucking teenager.

Who's got my fucking tobacco? Tea. Will somebody make some tea?

Maud Morning, Dad.

Patrick Where's my tobacco? Where the fuck is it?

Rose Have one of mine.

Patrick No, I want a decent smoke.

Patrick starts to deconstruct an armchair and to tear apart long-buried dog-ends to make a roll-up cigarette.

Lily That's what parasites do.

Patrick What?

Lily To the furniture.

John (*getting up now with his crumpled dinner suit minus jacket*) Hello. I'm John. How are you?

Patrick Dead, to all intents and purposes. Dead. I suffer from bad dreams. Excuse my *déshabillé*. You're not homosexual, are you?

John No.

Patrick Then it shouldn't bother you. Were you just in bed with Lily? I'm not passing judgement. She's over the age of consent.

Lily I was frightened. John stayed with me.

Patrick Good. There is too little kindness in the world . . .

Patrick is tearing more dog-ends apart.

Maud Dad. Don't do that. Have one of Rose's. Dad!

Patrick Terrible thing to embarrass your own children.

Do you mind if I smoke dog-ends, John?

John No. But there's some fresh tobacco in my jacket pocket there if you'd like it.

Patrick Thank you. Would you like a drink? (*He pours out whiskeys for himself and John and gives him a drink.*) I find the first is the sweetest before fluoride or domestic worries have set in. While the ghost of your body is still a warm imprint on your sheets.

John Thank you.

> *Patrick takes out John's tobacco and starts making a roll-up. Looking for a light, he pulls out a large bag of weed.*

Patrick What's this?

John It helps me to relax. Would you like some?

Patrick No, no, you're all right. I might try a bit sometime.

John Take it. Please. I've loads more. It's very nice. Strong.

Patrick (*looking at it and sniffing it*) That's very kind of you. The last time I possessed something like this was thirty years ago in Denver. Searching for Kerouac. I wanted to see the midget auto-racers. I didn't know if it was the cars that were midget or the people who drove them. Godforsaken place, Denver. A man stared out of a window and he was wanking – well, each to his own, but it was not such stuff as dreams are made on. What are you doing, Lily?

Lily (*taking out shoe polish and cloths*) I'm going to clean John's shoes.

John I'll do that.

Patrick Put the fucking shoes down. We were worried about you, John.

John Why?

Patrick We expected you to become one of the family on Tuesday.

John I couldn't leave London until yesterday. Did you not get the message?

Patrick No message arrived. People will steal anything these days. I walked into a café the other day to use the telephone. Never mind what for, I mean it was to make a call, but never mind who to. And sellotaped to the wall above the directories was a notice in biro. It said: 'No talking to imaginary strangers.' That's what the sign said. Because we are the loneliest and nearest to hell that we have ever been. Yet the western world smells so sanitised. It should smell like Golgotha. It should stink of rotting human flesh and pus and shit. But instead it smells like a McDonald's toilet. Do you ever frequent those hell-holes, John?

John I don't.

Patrick Good. I only ever enter them to defecate. My personalised gift to their corporation. Their cubicles have a consistent smell. That of a child's perfume and burnt skin. You can imagine the most terrible abominations going on in those red-and-yellow shitehouses. Have you eaten? Judith could make you a sandwich.

John I'm fine, thanks.

Judith I've got to go. See you all later.

Patrick I agree. Eating is a waste of time.

Maud See you.

John Goodbye.

Lily Will you see Esther?

Patrick Fuck's sake. She's in London, Lily. She's been there fifteen years. Remember?

Lily I do remember. I just forget.

Patrick Well, stop forgetting.

Judith See you. (*Judith exits.*)

Patrick Why did you ask to stay here, John, and not in a hotel?

John I wanted to stay somewhere quiet.

Patrick Do you not think that quiet is a state of mind?

Lily People die in hotels.

John They do. I should go and look at my script.

Patrick One of the girls will show you the cottage.

Maud We're not prostitutes, Patrick.

Patrick I asked you to show him the cottage, not fuck him. Sharper than a serpent's tooth. Do you know where that is from, John?

John *King Lear.*

Patrick He had three daughters too, didn't he? I feel for him. No wonder he went fucking mad. And that was without the mother-in-law. Will somebody show John his bed?

Rose Will you come with me, John?

John Thank you for the dance, Lily.

Patrick You have no bag? No trappings?

John They're at the pub.

*Rose and John leave to go next door to the cottage,
which adjoins the kitchen.*

Lily It's better than a hotel because hotels have upside-
down glasses in the bathroom to scare you.

Patrick What the fuck is scary about an upside-down
glass?

Lily Because you can imagine yourself inside is why.
Tiny and scratching at the sides and no one hearing you.

Rose's room. Rose and John enter.

Rose There's nothing to show, really. Bed. Window.
Floor. Do you need anything?

John No. This is perfect.

Rose Towels are in the cupboard.

John Thanks. Is this your room?

Rose Yeah.

John So where will you stay?

Rose Upstairs. It's nice, all of us sharing for a bit. Shall
I get you some tea or something?

John No. Thank you.

Rose I'll put the fire on. (*She switches on an electric
fire.*)

John Thanks. (*He gets out a hip-flask and has a swig of
vodka.*) Would you like some? Russia's finest?

Rose Thanks. (*He pours her a little into a glass on the
bedside table.*) That's strong.

John It's the real thing. From Moscow.

Rose Were you there?

John I did a film there about the poet Esenin.

Rose Do you always play writers?

John And criminals. What do you do?

Rose I work at a bookie's . . . temporarily. I've a couple of weeks off while it's being refurbished. But I've got to find a different job.

John You don't like it?

Rose I hate it. Plus it's dangerous. There's been two hold-ups in the last three years.

John In such a small town?

Rose People pass through. Was Lily okay with you last night?

John She was great.

Rose It was good of you to be with her. I didn't realise she was frightened.

John I don't think she was. She just wanted a bit of company. Do you mind if I smoke in here?

Rose No.

John Thank you.

He offers Rose a cigarette, which she accepts.

Rose Thanks. (*She passes him a religious-looking ashtray.*)

John You went to Lourdes?

Rose Lily's sister Kitty. She used to go there every year. Did you see her in the front room?

John No.

Rose She's on the mantelpiece. Her ashes. So do you know your lines?

John Most of them.

Rose You're playing Yeats?

John I am.

Rose That's a nice part to play. (*Pause.*) Isn't it?

John It is.

Rose I'll leave you to it. Are you tired?

John Exhausted.

Rose You've cut your hand. It looks quite deep.

John Yes . . . I don't know how I did that.

Rose Do you want a plaster?

John No. It's fine.

Rose I'll get you one. There's some in the bathroom.

Rose goes into the adjoining bathroom.

John (*to Rose in the bathroom*) Thank you. I like your room.

Rose (*from the bathroom*) It's all right. It's nice in the morning . . . gets the sun. All the cats congregate on the roof out there.

She returns with a wet towel, TCP, cotton wool and a plaster and places them next to John.

You should clean your cut.

John I should.

Rose Are you filming tomorrow?

John Yes . . . unless it rains.

Rose Are you all right?

John Yes.

Rose We're in if you need anything.

John Is there a clock in here?

Rose No. I'll get you one.

John I forgot to pack one. My mother died.

Rose Your mother?

John Yes. On Tuesday.

Rose God. I'm sorry. Had she been ill?

John Yes. She was very ill. Very ill.

Rose And they expect you to work still?

John They shifted scenes round me for a couple of days.
So I could stay for the funeral.

Rose I'm sorry.

John No. I'm sorry. I'm not quite sure where I am or
what I'm doing.

Rose Course you're not. Give me your hand. (*She cleans
his cut, puts a plaster on it and holds his hand.*)

John Thank you.

Rose You should be with your family.

John No. Probably best to work.

Rose Get some sleep.

John Yes, I will. Sorry.

Rose Don't be sorry.

*She takes her hand away and John curls up on the
bed. Rose takes a blanket from the cupboard and puts
it on him.*

Are you warm enough? Shall I get you more blankets?

John No thank you.

Rose Shall I draw the curtains?

John Yes, please.

Rose Are you all right on your own?

John I think so. I don't really know.

Rose Shall I stay with you a while?

John Yes. Please.

Rose sits on the bed and takes his hand.

Thank you.

She curls up next to him.

Thank you . . .?

Rose Rose.

John Rose.

They lie together.

SCENE FIVE

*The Library, the same morning. Judith is sorting through
a pile of books. Gary walks in and bangs down a pile of
books.*

Gary This is a hold-up. Give me all your Dostoevskys.

Judith Hi, Gary. Do any of these want renewing?

Gary I don't believe in it. I had a drink with your actor fella.

Gary handles the books on the desk. One is large with a mirror-type cover that reflects one's face.

Is this a book or a mirror?

Judith Self-help.

Gary I don't think it would help me. Staring into that. (*handling several Yeats books*) You reading Yeats?

Judith I thought that John might be interested in them.

Gary Do you remember when we did Yeats at school? Everyone laughed because Miss Cooper read from his diaries about him being celibate for seven years? (*reading from one of the books*) 'Half-close your eyelids, loosen your hair.' Do you think she did?

Judith You look tired.

Gary You look beautiful. You didn't hear or see me last night, did you?

Judith No. Are you in trouble? What have you done?

Gary Nothing. Only I walked John up to yours after the pub chucked us out. You were sat in the dark by your window. I watched you. I was going to climb up to you but I thought you'd laugh. And the wall was very wet.

Judith You tried to climb up?

Gary For a moment. I was drunk. Then I just looked up at you.

Judith What did I look like?

Gary Very beautiful. Sad. Incredibly young.

Judith I wouldn't have laughed at you.

Gary No?

Judith No. I was asleep. It was Rose you were staring at.

Gary Rose?

Judith She's staying in my room while John's here.

Gary I assumed it was you . . . (*He starts to walk out.*)

Judith Gary . . .

Gary What? What is it, Judith Kennedy? What do you want?

Judith What? It's not my fault you were chatting up my sister. I wanted to ask you something. Are you busy next Friday?

Gary I'm going away next week.

Judith Where to?

Gary London. To live. What do you think?

Judith I think that's great.

Gary Do you?

Judith I do.

Gary What did you want to ask me?

Judith Nothing. What'll you do there?

Gary I've a few games lined up.

Judith Where will you stay?

Gary There's a room come up at Liam's. Will you come and see me over there?

Judith Maybe. Will you send me a postcard?

Gary Never liked them. They always seemed a bit public. See you.

Judith Will you bring all your books back tomorrow?

Gary Possibly . . . Can I not keep them as past services rendered to the library?

Gary exits and Judith sits down.

SCENE SIX

Rose's room. Rose and John are in bed naked. Rose pulls the sheets over her.

John Are you all right?

Rose Yes. You?

John Yeah. (*He reaches over to his cigarettes and lights one. He offers one to Rose.*)

Rose Thanks.

Pause.

John Getting dark outside.

Rose Yeah.

John The days are very short.

Rose Yeah.

John The sound of the rain is nice.

Rose It is.

John Do you have to go?

Rose No. Do you want me to go?

John No.

Rose Can I ask you something?

John Anything.

Pause.

Rose Did you love your mother?

John Yes. I think so.

Rose Did you see her when she was dead?

John Yes. Twice. First at the hospital.

Rose What was that like?

John Horrible. I wanted to lift her out of the bed and carry her home through the park.

Rose But you didn't?

John No. No, I didn't. Then I saw her in the Chapel of Rest.

Rose How was that?

John Grim. She looked like a man who had put on too much blue eye-shadow. Terrible smell. Like the labs at my old school.

Rose Did you feel angry?

John No. I wanted sex. I wanted to find someone on the street and fuck them. I got porn videos out and spent the night watching them. Wanking. One was set in a hospital. Am I going to hell?

Rose No. If I saw my mother dead I'd feel absolutely indifferent. Am I going to hell?

John No.

Rose gets up and finds various garments and shoes around and in the bed. She starts to get dressed.

John You've got a beautiful body.

Rose Have I?

John You have.

Rose You're my first lover, John.

John I'm not?

Rose Course you're not. I just thought it sounded nice. I like your nose.

John My nose?

Rose Your eyes and everything too. But you seem to think with your nose.

John Makes me sound a bit like a spaniel.

Rose You are a bit like a spaniel. They're nice.

John Not particularly heroic though, are they?

Rose They are. They go splashing into ponds without thinking and they race around after sticks.

John Is that your idea of heroic, Rose?

Rose They're fearless.

John And a bit stupid.

Rose No they're not. I like your jawline too. I like the way it curves here . . . (*touching his jaw*) Are you still aching? For more sex?

John It's . . . a pretty strong ache.

She puts her hand under the sheet, touches him.

Rose Is that making it any better?

John That's helping. That's helping a lot.

Rose continues . . .

Rose There?

John Yes. Just there.

Rose So you don't like spaniels?

John I think they're . . . fantastic.

Rose But stupid.

John No. I think they're phenomenally intelligent. Hugely . . . hugely cerebral creatures . . . oh yes . . . very very . . . very . . . yes . . . yes.

Rose kisses John and starts to take her clothes off.

SCENE SEVEN

The kitchen. Maud, Patrick and Lily are watching the TV.

Maud Can we put the sound up?

Lily It's my house and it's my turn and I like the sound down.

Patrick It's no use trying to reason with a lunatic.

Lily I'm not lunatic. I'm selective. I'm going to ask John to come to the beach with me tomorrow. Do you think he'll come?

Patrick He's here to make a film not fucking sandcastles.

Judith comes in from outside.

Judith Hiya. John not here?

Lily He's taking me to the beach tomorrow.

Judith What's this? (*She sits down to watch it with them.*)

Maud Robert Mitchum. Speechless.

Lily John's taking me to the beach tomorrow. He promised.

Patrick You haven't even fucking asked him yet.

Judith Who's taking you?

Patrick I'm not.

Maud I can't. I've got to revise.

Rose enters from outside.

Lily Rose will take me. You'll take me, won't you, Rose?

Rose Take you where?

Maud Where did you go?

Rose Into town.

Lily To the beach. With John. Tomorrow.

Maud What did you go into town for?

Rose I needed to buy something. I think he'll be working, Lily.

Maud So where is it?

Rose What? Oh, they didn't have it.

Lily Why have you no coat? You'll become an Inuit.

Rose What are you watching?

Patrick Fuck knows.

Rose Why are you up, Dad?

Patrick My room smelt of earth. I thought I'd take John down the Pegasus. Introduce him to Gifford and the boys. Is someone making tea? Judith?

Judith gets up to make the tea.

Lily Will you take me, Rose?

Rose Yeah, we'll get the bus. Just the two of us.

Maud He doesn't look like Yeats. He's much better-looking. Don't tell him I said that. Is he married, do you think?

Lily He doesn't smell married to me.

Maud What does a married man smell like?

Lily Like rubber. And their necks are thicker than John's.

Maud Did Grandad smell like rubber?

Patrick He smelt like Jamesons.

Lily The bastard stank of rubber.

There is a knock on the door. John enters.

Patrick No need to knock, John. Not unless it's for dramatic effect. Will you eat with us?

John I don't want to put you to any trouble.

Patrick You're not. I never cook. The girls are dying to know if you're married.

Maud We are not. Nobody said that.

Patrick Are you beholden to somebody back at the OK Corral? Are they waiting to see you ride back through the sunset? Maud thinks you're much better-looking than Yeats. Which is not a great feat. He had a very weak chin, didn't he? He should have grown a beard.

John What are you watching? Robert Mitchum?

Patrick *Night of the Hunter* . . . the silent version.

John Is there something wrong with the telly?

Patrick No. With Lily.

Lily Would you like the sound up, John?

*She goes to the television and turns the sound up. The
dialogue on screen is about love and hate.*

Maud Rose, you've been all around town with your
jumper on inside out.

Rose Who wants a drink?

Maud You, I should think.

Rose gets a bottle of whiskey out and downs a glass.

Rose Dad? John?

Lily What about me?

Rose Would you like one?

Lily No.

Patrick (*indicating the television*) You must stay and eat,
John, else you'll never know if good prevailed over evil.
Now that you're one of the family you must be a part of
our rituals. Then you can come on down to the pub.
Meet Gifford.

Maud Don't say yes if he asks you for an arm-wrestle.

Patrick And I'll introduce you to an angel with the
biggest . . .

Judith Stay. Eat.

John I will if that's not a problem.

Patrick There are no problems in this house. Only
disasters. Goodbye, progeny. I'll see you in a bit, John.

John See you there.

Judith 'Bye, Patrick.

Maud 'Bye, Dad. Spy on Kevin for me if he's there.

Patrick Goodnight, Lily. Remember me at my best.

Lily (*quietly*) Fuck off.

Rose 'Bye, Dad . . .

Judith I brought you some books about Yeats. I work at the library. You might have them already. But there's lots of pictures. (*She hands John the books.*)

John That's very thoughtful. Very kind. I've not seen these before.

Lily If we're going to have the sound up then we're not allowed to talk. Except for John. And except for me. Or if someone catches on fire.

They sit and watch the film silently for a few moments.

John?

John Yes.

Lily Do you have plans for tomorrow?

John We're filming. Unless it rains.

Lily What time are the buses, Rose?

They sit as more dialogue about love comes over the screen.

SCENE EIGHT

Rose and John are on the beach. It is raining. Lily is having a pee nearby, out of sight.

Lily (*shouting, from out of sight*) Rose! It's coming out of me like a horse!

Rose (*to Lily*) Great. You let me know when you're finished.

Lily (*out of sight*) It's like the yellow rivers of Babylon . . .

Rose Shall I come over?

Lily I want no help.

Rose I'm sorry if Lily was insistent about today.

John She wasn't. She just said that I'd promised to come here with her and that she was probably going to die very soon.

Rose I'm sorry.

John Don't be. It's great here.

Lily (*out of sight*) Do you want to pee now, Rose?

Rose (*to Lily*) No.

John You were very wild and kind yesterday.

Rose You were very fucking sexy. Subject closed.

Lily (*approaching*) Which subject? Were you watching the birds?

John Yes. They're wonderful.

Lily Shall we come here again tomorrow?

Rose We can't.

Lily I might come on my own. I'm going to collect some shells. Shall we make a fire?

Rose I think the wood might be too damp.

Lily I'm a bit scared.

Rose Of what?

Lily That you won't let me come here on my own tomorrow. Rose, I'm scared.

Rose What are you scared of?

Lily (*upset*) I'm scared that John thinks I'm stupid. I'm scared that you two want to be alone together and that you'll go away and leave me here. And I'll become the size of a pebble and someone will step on me.

Rose Give me your hand.

Lily What if you're asking for my hand and you want to hold John's? You hold Rose's other hand, John . . . Those birds sound like they're hurting. Everything sounds like it's in pain. Forgive me.

Rose For what?

Lily Anything. Please.

Rose Of course.

Lily I have told lies.

Rose We all tell lies.

Lily Am I ill?

Rose Do you feel ill?

Lily One minute I'm full and the next minute I'm empty. I'm freezing. Is it cold or is it me?

John It is cold. Would you like a coffee? Tea?

Lily Yes, please. Coffee, please. White. Two sugars. Can I have a cake too? From the sad man in the van?

John Of course. Do you want a coffee, Rose?

Rose I'd love one. Thanks.

John goes off to get some coffees.

Lily I should go away and leave you both. I'll go for a walk with my cake. My legs are like those maps we felt at school. Why are you sad?

Rose I'm not.

Lily Scared?

Rose No.

Lily Of John?

Rose No. Why do you say that?

Lily Your hands are trapped.

Rose Really?

Lily Yes. You want to hold his hand?

Rose I don't know what I want.

Lily You want a paradise on earth and you don't want to live in paradise alone.

Rose Yes.

Lily I lied to your mother. When she was little. I told her that everything was going to be like a fairy tale. I said that she would go to parties all the time. She's not dead, is she? My Esther?

Rose No. She's not dead, Nan.

Lily No. Me neither. Do you want to fuck John?

Rose Shut up, Lily.

Lily The question is a fair one.

Rose Be quiet.

Lily Don't address me as though I were a child. I have had men inside me. And children. Don't put me in a cot.

John comes back with the coffees.

You bought everything, John. Don't the cakes and crisps look nice together? I'm going to collect some shells and find some feathers. Don't drink my coffee. Or touch my Wagon Wheel.

Lily leaves Rose and John. She sings the sailor song from Thief of Baghdad *as she walks away*

John She looks about ten years old.

Rose She says she wakes up and feels a different age every day. That the concept of time means nothing to her now so she has no fear of death. Have you spoken to your family today?

John No. I haven't. I've just been going over the script.

Rose Is it good?

John Terrible.

Rose So who's playing Maud Gonne?

John Anjelica Ryan?

Rose Is she Irish?

John Californian.

Rose Do you know her?

John No. Apparently she's a bit neurotic. Her agent has written a thesis on what she can and can't show in the sex scenes.

Rose I thought those two never had sex.

John They do in this film. Frequently. Always near swans.

Lily approaches humming 'Isn't this a lovely day to be caught in the rain?'

Lily Where's my Wagon Wheel? It's raining onto the sea. The patterns are terribly pretty. I have no womb, John.

They took it out. How long will you stay with us?

John Six weeks.

Lily I'll be sad when you leave. I know a poem. 'I was a
child and she was a child in our kingdom by the sea.' We
learnt that at school. He loved her and she died. Do me
a poem, John. From your film.

John What sort of poem?

Lily Anything as long as it's short. I'll close my eyes and
imagine it.

John
A mermaid found a swimming lad,
Picked him for her own,
Pressed her body to his body,
Laughed; and plunging down
Forgot in cruel happiness
That even lovers drown.

Lily Is it finished? I called Esther a mermaid because
we made her on the beach. Let's have a dance. I used to
win competitions with my sister Kitty. My husband used
to share me and Kitty on the dance floor, John. And
sometimes in the bedroom too. You two dance and I'll
do the music.

Rose I'm fine, Lily. You dance.

Lily Dance with me, John.

*They start to dance. Lily starts to hum 'Isn't this a
lovely day?' and sings it, and Fred Astaire's version of
'Isn't this a lovely day?' joins in.*

Come and dance with us.

Rose You're all right. I like watching you two.

Lily What do you think we are? Performing fucking monkeys? Get off your ass, you miserable fucking spinster. Get up and fucking dance with us.

They all dance together.

SCENE NINE

The Pegasus. Patrick is finishing a pint. Judith approaches him.

Patrick What are you doing here?

Judith I live up the road.

Patrick Are you pregnant?

Judith No. Do you want another drink?

Patrick Jamesons. You sit. I'll go to the bar. What are you having?

Judith No, you're fine. I'll get them.

Patrick Don't deprive me of my vigil.

Judith (*looking to the bar at Nikki*) Oh, right. Is that a bikini she's got on?

Patrick It's a halterneck top.

Judith You're very well informed.

Patrick I asked her the same question earlier. What's Gifford doing sniffing round the bar?

Judith What's he done to his hand?

Patrick Tried to catch the moon. What'll you have?

Pause.

It's not a difficult question.

Pause.

Judith I've been thinking I might go and see Mum.

Pause.

Patrick Good.

Judith I might go on Friday. For a week. What do you think?

Patrick Have you bought your ticket?

Judith I have, yeah.

Patrick Then why ask me my opinion?

Judith Do you mind?

Patrick Why would I mind?

Rose Do you think I should?

Patrick Are you asking me if she'll be pleased to see you?

Judith Maybe.

Patrick Since when did I become the fucking oracle?

Judith You don't think I should go.

Patrick I don't think people should get up in the mornings. I don't think people should be allowed to talk to each other. Let alone affect each others' lives or decisions. I think people should live in isolation wards, not streets. (*He starts to move towards the bar.*)

Judith Shall I still stay for a drink?

Patrick Do as you will. You're not a child.

Patrick goes to the bar. Judith sits.

SCENE TEN

*The kitchen. Rose is sitting near the fire, drinking wine.
Late. There is a knock on the door. John enters.*

Rose You don't have to knock. How was your dinner?

John Usual rubbish. Mostly about Anjelica and therapy
and her new-found relationship with Maud.

Rose Is the director nice?

John Very nice.

Rose You finished late?

John Yeah. Can I sit down for a minute?

Rose Course you can. Do you want some wine?

*John sits and takes off his scarf. Maud walks in,
drunk, from outside.*

Maud Has Kevin been here?

Rose No. I thought you were both at the Pegasus.

Maud We were . . . Oh shit.

Rose What is it?

Maud I thought he'd be here . . . I threw my pint over
him.

Rose Why?

Maud Oh fuck.

Rose What?

Maud He says to me, 'Relationships change, don't they?'

Rose Yeah?

Maud Yeah. First they're great, then they're shit.

Rose You said that to him?

Maud No. But I kept asking him why he was distracted. He says, 'Oh it's politics,' and I know he's staring at Nikki's tits across the bar . . . then he has a go at me for getting a round in for everyone.

Rose Why?

Maud We're meant to be saving for Moscow. To visit descendants of Bakunin.

Rose Right.

Maud I've got to find him. I want to explode and there's no point unless he's there to hear it. Make him stay here if he comes. Will you?

Rose I will.

Maud exits.

Have you met Kevin?

John Yes. He talked to me about the film industry and explained to me how and why I was a prostitute.

Rose Will you have some wine?

Lily walks in.

Lily Who came home?

Rose Maud. Are you all right, Lily?

Lily (*upset*) I dreamt I had a baby but I forgot to feed it and its stomach became like a drum then I found it on a table and it was dead. I want to speak to Esther.

Rose The phone broke. Do you remember?

Lily I do. Patrick smashed it because Judith kept trying to ring London.

John Phone her on my mobile. I'll get it.

Lily Can I? 0044-208-493-6850. Thank you, John. Can I ring her from your room?

John Course you can.

Lily Will you take my hand?

Lily and John exit holding hands. Rose goes to the window and watches them go next door. She takes John's scarf from the back of his chair, smells it and puts it around her. She sits by the fire with her wine.

SCENE ELEVEN

The Pegasus. Judith and Patrick have had a few drinks together.

Judith Are you still angry with her?

Patrick No. No, I'm not.

Judith Do you still hate her?

Patrick I never hated her. I cut up her dresses but I never hated her.

Judith I thought you did.

Patrick It was a strange time.

Judith You told me one night that you raped her.

Patrick When did I say that?

Judith About a year after she'd gone.

Patrick You didn't believe me, did you?

Judith No. Why did you say it?

Patrick There were many times when I found myself geographically placed on top of your mother and I knew that she didn't want me there. That's probably what I meant.

Judith Do you remember that row we had? You said I'd grow up to be a 'fucking schoolteacher'.

Patrick I wasn't far wrong, was I?

Judith That was a bastard thing to say to a fifteen-year-old.

Patrick I was a bastard. I am a bastard.

Judith I should get some Taytos for Lily.

Patrick I found it painful that we grew distant.

Judith We didn't grow distant.

Patrick Didn't we? When Esther left you became obsessed with keeping the place tidy. You'd watch me with my wine and cigarettes, waiting for my ash to fall.

Judith I didn't.

Patrick My heart was hewn in two and you were worried about a fucking wine stain.

Judith You were all over the place.

Patrick We used to know each other. We grew apart.

Judith We still know each other.

Patrick No . . . Damage happened way before your mother left.

Judith What damage?

Patrick When you were eleven years old. You changed. You stopped being a child and you changed.

Judith Of course I changed.

Patrick Your heart changed but you denied it.

Judith I didn't feel anything less. Just differently.

Patrick I didn't like differently.

Judith I didn't like drunk.

Patrick That was me. That is me. I drink. I'd be the most miserable boring fucking bastard on the planet if I didn't. I'd be like the Ancient fucking Mariner. I'd corner you and start telling you something. You'd escape and when you came back in I'd resume from exactly where I left off. I'd be a bigger bully than I am now. I was scared of you, Judith.

Judith Scared of me?

Patrick I'm sorry. I didn't want to be. I always felt like you were waiting for me to fuck up. You always wanted to be right and I was always the villain.

Judith That's not fair. Not fair, Dad. I just wanted you to tell me that things were okay. And that you liked me. That was all I wanted. You were a bully. You didn't hit Mum. You didn't hit us. But everything was so black or white. We were on your side or we weren't. We hated the system or we didn't. And you were always pissed and threatening to kill yourself. You were scared of me?

Patrick I was a terrible fucking father.

Judith You weren't. It was a difficult time.

Patrick Am I a bully?

Judith No, you're not.

Patrick A tyrant, then?

Judith No.

Patrick I'm sorry.

Judith For what?

Patrick I'm just very sorry that I have not served you better.

Judith You've been brilliant.

Patrick Don't defend me, Judith. This is my apology. In response to your attack.

Judith It wasn't an attack.

Patrick It wasn't a fucking love song. It's good that you say these things. I wish you'd said them at the time.

Judith I wasn't strong enough at the time.

Patrick No. I'm sorry if I was a bully.

Judith You weren't . . .

Patrick I probably was. Forgive me. Please. Forgive me, for fuck's sake.

Judith All right. All right. I forgive you.

Patrick Did I just bully you into forgiving me?

Judith No. I forgave you of my own free will.

Patrick When you were born, Esther kept bursting into tears saying she was scared she'd have to take you back. The yard was a paradise. Summertime. She'd sing to you. I'd roll her a cigarette and we'd all just lie there on a blanket. And I'd watch the smoke curling up from my hand and I thought, fuck, this is heaven. I'll get those drinks. Whiskey?

Judith I can't. I've got work tomorrow.

Patrick One more will do no harm.

Judith I'll have an orange.

Patrick Have a real drink. Judith, my child, my first-born. You've never been drunk, have you? In all your . . . how many years?

Judith Thirty, Dad. No I haven't. And I've no desire to. I'm going home.

Patrick Don't go. I'm sorry . . . I thought we might be gypsies for a night. Get slaughtered, plastered together. I'm sorry . . . I don't want another one either. I'll walk you home. (*He gets up.*)

Judith A pint of Guinness and a double whiskey, no ice.

Patrick Really? Shall we get drunk? You have to remember I'm a fool. I know not what I do sometimes.

Judith Am I meant to say that I'm a fool too now?

Patrick That would be a sort of drunken patois etiquette. I say something. You agree and emphasise it or you wildly disagree and we have an arm-wrestle.

Judith Okay, I'm a fool too. Sometimes.

Patrick You're the most beautiful fool I've ever seen.

Judith Thanks, Dad.

Patrick Have I upset you? You look sad.

Judith No. I thought you were getting the drinks.

Patrick I go. I go. See how I fucking go. Shakespeare, that is. Did you know that?

Judith I didn't.

Patrick See. I can still teach you things. I love you.

Judith Yeah. I know.

Patrick I'll get the drinks. (*He goes to the bar.*)

SCENE TWELVE

The kitchen. Late. Rose has drunk most of the bottle of wine. John enters.

Rose Did she get through?

John Yes. They're talking now.

Rose She's talking to Mum?

John Yes.

Rose Thanks for looking after Lily. Your drink's there.

John I'd better go to bed.

Rose Oh right. 'Night.

John 'Night.

Rose 'Night. Sweet dreams.

John Thanks . . . Rose . . .

Rose Yeah?

John Sleep well.

John exits. Rose stares into the fire.

Rose Do you see the dragon there, Mum? That long spark is his tail. And there's a woman. And a man there too. She's got her arms stretched out towards him . . . but I can't see what the man's doing. I can't see what he's doing.

We see John in his room. He walks in and goes to the bathroom to put water on his face. When he comes back into the bedroom he lights a cigarette. From the same jeans pocket that he takes his lighter, he takes a small piece of paper. He looks at it and burns it. Then puts his lighter back into this pocket. Then he lies on his bed and smokes. In the kitchen Rose switches on the record player. 'Night and Day' plays, it is scratched and jumps . . . Rose sits by the fire and listens . . .

Like the beat beat beat of the tom tom
When the jungle shadows fall . . .
So a voice within me keeps repeating
You . . . you . . . you . . . you . . . you . . . you . . .
  you . . . you . . . you . . .

SCENE THIRTEEN

Outside in a lane. Patrick is kneeling in a ditch, looking at the star-filled sky. Judith stands by him.

Judith You okay, Dad?

Patrick I'm just having a look.

Judith At the sky? Are you all right?

Patrick I am. Are you cold? Do you want my coat, 'cos it's fucking freezing out here.

Judith No no. You're all right.

  Patrick starts to take his coat off.

Patrick I think you should wear this coat.

Judith No, you keep it on you. Are you getting up, Dad?

Patrick No. You see those fucking stars? Do you see them? Come here.

Judith I can see them from here. Are you getting up?

Patrick No. I'm in a position of worship. Come and kneel with me. Come on.

Judith Dad . . .

Patrick Don't worry about your tights. I'll buy you some new tights. Sit on my coat.

Judith No no. You're all right. (*Judith kneels down with him.*)

Patrick What do you think?

Judith Beautiful.

Patrick Better from down here, isn't it?

Judith It's beautiful.

Patrick Can you see the Great Bear? Can you?

Judith No.

Patrick No. Nor can I. Do you know what it looks like?

Judith No.

Patrick Me neither . . . those pictures of the constellations . . . they don't make sense . . . you get three stars in a triangle and a great big fucking eagle drawn around it with feathers and claws and a snake in its beak. Are you having a nice time?

Judith I am. I knocked a table over. Dad, I don't know if I can get up. Everything's spinning.

Patrick Just wait a moment. I'll get you up. Don't move.

Judith I won't. I can't. Thanks.

Patrick gets up and helps Judith to her feet. He takes her arm.

Patrick Can you walk all right?

Judith I don't know. I don't know anything. I'd like to see Gary. I really would.

Patrick Shall I take you to him?

Judith No . . . Could you, Dad? I don't know if I can walk.

Patrick Come here. You see? I can be useful.

He kneels down and gives her a piggy-back. He walks off with Judith on his back.

You tell me if you see any snakes.

'I Only Have Eyes For You' starts to play:

Are the stars out tonight?
I can't tell if it's cloudy or bright
'Cos I only have eyes for you, dear . . .

Interval.

Act Two

SCENE ONE

The kitchen. Later the same night. Rose is sitting drinking, while writing and listening to Marlene Dietrich's 'Lola'. There are screwed-up pages of a letter she is trying to write. Patrick crashes into something outside, glass smashes and he enters cursing, he has red on his hands and what looks like a black silk scarf around his neck. Rose abandons her letter and throws all the drafts into the fire. Patrick tries to fix himself a drink.

Rose Are you all right, Dad?

Patrick I need no assistance.

Rose Did you have a nice evening?

Patrick Nice is not a word I like to encourage.

Rose What have you done to your hand?

Patrick 'Blood. It will have blood.'

Rose Did you cut yourself?

Patrick No. Someone else.

Rose Have you been in a fight?

Patrick Since the day I was born.

Rose What happened, Dad?

Patrick There was no struggle. She came quietly.

Rose Dad . . .

Patrick Don't be scared, Rosie. I covered my tracks.

Rose Are you in trouble?

Patrick Very deep. Very dark. Are we alone? No, we're together . . . Groucho Marx . . .

Lily enters, abstracted.

Lily Did you bring Esther home with you?

Patrick No.

Lily Is she not here?

Patrick 'She wasn't here again today. Oh how I wish she'd go away.' Why did you name your daughter after a whore?

Lily What?

Patrick Esther. Ishtar. The whore of all whores.

Maud enters, sleepy and post-tearful.

Maud Judith's not come home. (*seeing his hands*) What's that? You been out with Gifford?

Patrick No. I've been painting. The town. Red.

Lily What have you got around your neck?

Patrick A scarf.

Lily No it's not.

Patrick A noose.

Rose Shall I take you to your room, Dad?

Patrick Like you took John to his room?

Rose What?

Maud Come on, Dad.

Maud helps him to stand up.

Patrick I'm not a child. And I'm not blind. 'Why, what could she have done, being what she is? Was there another Troy for her to burn?'

They exit.

SCENE TWO

Gary's flat. 4 a.m. Judith is sleeping, still drunk and out of it. Gary comes in with some water for her. Judith suddenly wakes.

Judith Rose!

Gary Judith. It's me.

Judith Gary . . . Gary, I thought I was somewhere else.

Gary Where were you?

Judith In a cellar. With Rose.

Gary Do you want some water?

Judith Yeah. Why am I here?

Gary I kidnapped you. Patrick and you were in the pub and I threw you over my shoulder and brought you home with me.

Judith No you didn't.

Gary Drink . . . it'll make you feel better tomorrow.

Judith Gary, I'm wearing foreign clothes. Where are mine?

Gary I hid them as part of my hostage plan.

Judith Where are they?

Gary They need washing. I'll take them to the launderette.

Judith What did I do? How did I get here?

Gary Patrick brought you.

Judith I was in a ditch with Dad talking about bears . . .

Gary You're all right. You've been a bit sick.

Judith No? What time is it? Should I be at work?

Gary It's four in the morning. You were having a nightmare.

Judith I stabbed Rose. She was bleeding to death and I did nothing. And I was hoping she'd die. Else she'd tell people it was me who killed her.

Gary Nobody's dead. Just drunk.

Judith Thanks, Gary. You look different.

Gary Different?

Judith God, it was horrible. I stood there watching her bleed onto the concrete floor. She was looking at me and she was in such pain.

Gary Was just a dream. Try to get some sleep now.

Judith curls up to sleep. Gary puts the blankets straight around her. Then he sits at a table with his chess set and account books.

SCENE THREE

Patrick's room. He is sitting on his bed, drink and roll-up in hand. He lights a candle and places it on a chair. He takes the black slip from around his neck, puts it on a clothes hanger and hangs it from a shelf, then turns the light out, pours himself a drink and raises his glass to the slip. He sits opposite the slip, watches it, approaches it, touches it.

Patrick An angel was flying in the dark night and I smote her down. I stole her from her lifeline and I wrapped her around my neck and nobody knew where she began and where I endeth. I salute you, patron silken saint of lost souls. I was in the desert and you gave me drink. You slaked my thirst. I was wracked on the wheel in the heat and you sang your gypsy song and gave me water. You have confused me. So perhaps I'm still alive. Terrifying thought. (*He laughs.*) It's very funny. No it is. (*He pours himself another drink.*)

SCENE FOUR

Rose's room, 4 a.m. John is in bed. Rose comes into the room. She is very drunk. She sits on the floor and watches him. She sits on the bed. He wakes.

John Shit!

Rose Did I wake you?

John God. What are you doing? What time is it?

Rose It's very early. Or very late. I wanted to see you.

John Right.

Rose Should I go?

John No. No . . . I'm just . . .

Rose You don't want me to stay, do you?

John Rose . . .

63

Rose It just felt like the right thing to come and see you.
I knew it was wrong too but I thought if the world was
going to end tomorrow and it really could because
everything is so fucked up . . . if it was going to end
tomorrow I'd choose to lie with you tonight. I'm drunk.
Do you mind?

John I don't mind. But . . .

Rose Do you think I'm a slut?

John No. Course not.

Rose I think you think I am.

John No. I really don't.

Rose I don't do that with people. Not much. It just felt
right.

John It was right. Very right.

Rose But it's not right any more?

John It's complicated.

Rose Why?

John What happened was . . .

Rose . . . beautiful.

John It was.

Rose And pure. I mean we were very dirty but pure in
our dirtiness.

John We were.

Rose Should I go? I don't want to. I will but I don't
want to. Can I have a cigarette with you then I'll go?

John They're on the table.

Rose takes one from the pack on the bedside table.

Rose Do you have a light?

John (*indicating his jeans*) In my pocket.

Rose I know I shouldn't have come in. But we spend all our lives doing shoulds and shouldn'ts, don't we? I was going to say there was something I needed badly from my drawer, but I thought . . . I just think you're beautiful. I thought that when I first saw you. On the floor with Lily in a blanket. Like a couple of Red Indians. Sat there. I could imagine you running after horses. Then we were here together . . . . you . . . inside me. I felt it, you know? Very deep. And on the beach I wanted to cry because you were so kind to Lily and when we all danced it was nice, wasn't it? Dancing on the sand in the rain?

John It was. It was wonderful.

Rose I'm sorry. I shouldn't be here. This is your room.

John No. This is your room.

Rose I give it to you. Like I gave myself to you. I'll go after I've had a cigarette. I don't want to stop you from your sleep. You're fucking beautiful, do you know that?

John You're beautiful too.

Rose No. Sometimes. I felt beautiful in bed with you. And when I got up and collected my clothes I knew you were watching me. My arse. My back. And I knew you liked it. I shouldn't be saying this, should I?

John I did like it. I thought you looked gorgeous. You are very beautiful, Rose.

Rose No. Do you think Judith and Maud are beautiful?

John Yes. I suppose so.

Rose You don't or you do?

John Yes, I do.

Rose Who's the most beautiful?

John That's a bit silly.

Rose It's nice, though, isn't it? Being silly together? It's nice talking like this. So who is the most beautiful?

John You can't measure it like that.

Rose They can now. In America. They have a machine. It tells you who is the prettiest and who is the ugliest.

John Very useful.

Rose Should I go? No . . . Why should I go? You've only a holy ashtray to talk to. Shall I take you to another beach? There's beautiful beaches round here.

John That would be lovely. Sometime.

Rose Sorry. I'm drunk and you're not. I was just sitting by the fire, though, and it was so nice just drinking . . . thinking . . . drinking. Do you have a light?

John Jeans pocket.

Rose Thank you. For the light . . . I saw a programme about the ballerina Anna Pavlova. Do you know her?

John I've heard of her.

Rose She died. And she was meant to be dancing that night. In Paris. And everyone was there. All the musicians and the audience and everyone. All waiting for her. And then they got told she'd died. And do you know what they did?

John What did they do?

Rose (*becoming weepy with drink and emotion*) They did the whole thing . . . the whole ballet right from the beginning to the end with all the musicians and the dancers and they just shone a light where she was meant to be. They just shone one light and it moved round where she was meant to be dancing. And everyone watched the light and they knew she wasn't there but she was, you know? And I thought it was the most beautiful way to die in the world. (*crying*)

John (*putting his arm around her*) It was. It was.

Rose Sorry. I'll go in a minute. I'm sorry. It's all been a bit intense, you know? Did you ever feel that you were waiting for something and when it happened you couldn't handle it? It was too immense, too strange, or I don't know what. Do you? Do you know?

Rose feels in John's jeans pocket. She finds a pack of condoms as well as his lighter.

I thought you said you didn't have any.

John I didn't.

Rose You bought some?

John Yes.

Rose Today?

John Yes.

Rose And one of them's gone already.

John Rose . . .

Rose With the Californian?

John No. Somebody else.

Rose One of my sisters?

John No . . . Rose . . . nobody you know. I'm sorry.

Rose No. No. Don't be.

John I've upset you.

Rose I was upset before you got here. Just your coming here made me realise how upset I was. Goodnight.

John Rose. Come here. I'm sorry.

Rose Nothing's ever quite how you think it.

John I'm sorry.

Rose It's funny how you can surprise yourself, isn't it? I understand being surprised by other people, but to surprise your own self it's pretty fucking stupid, isn't it?

John I don't know.

Rose I do. It's incredibly fucking stupid. 'Night.

Rose walks out.

SCENE FIVE

Patrick's room. Dawn. Patrick is singing to the slip.

Patrick
'Down by the salley gardens my love and I did meet:
She passed the salley gardens with little snow-white feet.
She bid me take love easy, as the leaves grow on the
  tree:
But I, being young and foolish, with her would not
  agree.

In a field by the river my love and I did stand,
And on my leaning shoulder she laid her snow-white
  hand.
She bid me take life easy, as the grass grows on the
  weirs;
But I was young and foolish, and now am full of tears.'

68

SCENE SIX

Gary's flat. 10 a.m. Gary is sitting with his chess set and book. Judith is in bed.

Judith Morning.

Gary Morning. Do you want a game of chess?

Judith No.

Gary There's a cup of tea next to you. Should still be hot.

Judith Thanks. What time is it?

Gary Ten. I rang your work, said you were sick.

Judith What did they say?

Gary They hope you get very well very soon.

Judith I can't remember anything about getting here.

Gary You don't remember us having sex?

Judith We didn't.

Gary I was fantastic.

Judith Silly. Did I just crash out?

Gary No. You were talking about your mum. Then you kept asking why your dad would be scared of you. You cried and went to sleep.

Judith I vomit, then I weep. I'm sorry. How did we all end up here anyway?

Gary You told Patrick you wanted to see me.

Judith I'm sorry. Is this your shirt?

Gary No. It belongs to the woman I had to chuck out when you arrived.

Judith Were you asleep?

Gary No.

Judith I feel as if I've been in a fight. Can I stay here today? Am I in your way?

Gary No. You sleep as long as you want.

Judith That tea was good . . . You've not slept, have you?

Gary I'll sleep later. (*He gets out a notebook. He puts on a pair of glasses.*)

Judith What are you writing?

Gary I'm working something out.

Judith Have you some games booked in London?

Gary A few.

Judith When did you start wearing glasses?

Gary I just wear them for chess. Stops me getting headaches. And when I do the books. (*He moves a chess piece and writes the move down.*)

Judith Is it important that you win against yourself?

Gary Very. It's all about sacrifice and combination.

Judith Is it?

Gary Yeah . . . You have to set up a mating net. What do you reckon? Queen's Gambit or Kalashnikov Sicilian?

Judith They both sound pretty dangerous.

He moves a piece.

Which did you go for?

Gary Mm? I don't know yet.

Judith Do you remember when I first came round here? All you had was a striped mug and a mattress.

Gary And a tape recorder.

Judith I couldn't decide whether you were a poet or a murderer.

Gary I was both.

Judith You spent all your money on new sheets for when I came to stay the night and they were the wrong size.

Gary I don't remember that.

Judith You did. Could I have some water, please?

Gary brings her a glass of water.

Are you tired? You must be tired.

Gary I don't need much sleep.

Judith Come in with me. Sleep next to me.

Gary No. You're all right.

Judith Please.

Gary You want me to sleep next to you?

Judith No. (*He moves another piece and writes it down.*) Shall I tell you what I want?

Judith sits up on the bed.

Gary Yes.

Judith I want you to take off your clothes.

Pause. He tentatively starts to take off his shirt.

No. I want you to take off your clothes that are on me.

He takes off Judith's shirt.

71

Now I want you to take off your clothes that are on you.

Gary starts to take his clothes off.

Now I want you to kiss me.

He takes her head in his hands, which causes a severe pain.

Sorry, without moving my head too much. I'm trying to seduce you.

Gary I was getting that picture, yes.

Judith What do you think?

Gary I might not be able to. I'm a bit nervous. Do you mind?

Judith No. I don't mind, Gary.

They hold each other.

Gary Judith. Judith. Judith . . .

Judith Are you all right?

Gary Yes.

Judith kisses him.

Judith We can just hold each other, you know?

Gary No no no . . . I'll give it a try.

They embrace.

SCENE SEVEN

The kitchen. Lily and Maud are filling in Lily's diet sheet.

Lily Can I have a cup of tea? I feel as dry as Egypt.

Maud We've got to finish this, Lily. Judith'll have a fit if we've not done it again. Where did Rose go, anyway? I'm meant to be revising.

Lily My tongue cleaveth to my jaws.

Maud (*writing in the book*) What did you have for lunch?

Lily Slugs. I don't give a fuck. I just want a cup of tea. Why do they harangue and harass me, anyway? I'm going to die. So fucking what?

Maud They need to know if you have any allergies.

Lily I do. I have an allergy to diet sheets. Chuck it in the fire.

Maud Don't! That's a week's worth of journal.

Lily What difference if I ate peas before I died? Fuck it!

Lily and Maud have a tussle and the book gets torn. Lily feeds some pages into the fire.

Maud Shit.

Lily I want sex. Not iron pills. Good hard sex.

Maud I'll make the tea.

Patrick enters from upstairs. He is dressed smartly and starts to polish his shoes.

Maud You going somewhere, Dad? You want a cup of tea?

Lily Why is there ladies' underwear strewn in my yard?

Maud Do you want me to do that for you, Da?

Lily There are foreign clothes-pegs in the yard, Patrick.

Maud I'll do that for you, Da.

Lily Why are you anointing your shoes? It's not my funeral yet. You're just trying to scare me. You implied that Rose was a slut last night. And you took Judith out. You shouldn't have favourites. Am I your favourite? I'm John's favourite. (*She feeds her diet-sheet papers into the fire.*) 'Thou hast kept me alive, that I should not go down to the pit . . . What profit is there in my blood, when I shall go down to the pit? Shall the dust praise thee?'

Patrick leaves the house. Lily runs to the window to watch him go.

SCENE EIGHT

Gary's flat. Gary and Judith are in bed.

Judith You didn't seem particularly nervous to me.

Gary No. The nerves went. I got distracted and forgot about them.

Judith Was I distracting?

Gary Very. Was I?

Judith You were. Are you all right?

Gary I am. Are you having a nice day off work?

Judith I am.

Gary Is this what librarians do on their day off, is it?

Judith It is. We . . . we do some research into the outside world and then we write it all up and put it in a file in the reference section.

Gary Is it a file on the top shelf?

Judith It is.

Gary So that would mean you have to climb the ladder to put it away?

Judith Stop it.

Gary The library was vandalised last night, you know.

Judith It wasn't?

Gary There's red paint all over the wall. It says, 'Make as much noise as you fucking like . . . please!'

Judith No?

Gary Yeah.

Judith Hooligans. Do you think it was Kevin?

Gary No. I know who it was.

Judith Who was it?

Gary It was you and your dad.

Judith No. You're teasing me.

Gary No, I'm not. He said he was liberating the silence.

Judith God. I've become a drunk, a criminal and a harlot all in one night.

Gary It looks grand.

Judith Oh, Gary . . .

Gary It needed a bit of colour. You know what I used to like best about the library?

Judith What?

Gary When you'd say 'Shh' . . . I found it so fucking sexy. I'd stay in the reference section for ages just to hear you say it.

Judith You didn't? I thought you were there a lot. You were always noisy.

Gary To make you say 'Shh'. You want a cup of tea?

Judith Would you have to get up to make it?

Gary I would, yeah. I'd like to have an invention under my bed but all I've got's the kettle across the way.

Judith I'd love one.

Gary You be saying your Hail Marys while I'm making it. You've got a lot of them to do after last night and today.

Judith Shush . . .

Gary Don't you be doing that to me, Sister Judith. You know what effect that has upon a poor lost sinner like myself.

Judith Shh . . .

Gary Once more for while I'm in the kitchen.

Judith Shh.

They kiss. Gary half-dresses.

Judith When was the last time a woman inhabited these sheets? What? Who was it?

Gary Nikki. A few months ago.

Judith And before that?

Gary Stop it.

Judith I'm just curious.

Gary Last summer. A girl who played chess.

Judith Did she beat you? At chess.

Gary We didn't play.

Judith You spent the night together here? A few nights?

Gary Yes.

Judith Do you want to know my carnal history of the last few years?

Gary No. I don't want to know. I really really don't want to know. Thanks anyway. I'll get your tea. Do you want some toast?

Judith No. I've had no lovers since we parted. You're the only man I've known.

Gary Is that why you left me? Because you wanted to know other men?

Judith No.

Gary Why then?

Judith I didn't think you saw me as I really was.

Gary How did you think I saw you?

Judith As a sort of nun figure. In pain.

Gary Especially when you were on the library ladder. How do you think I see you now?

Judith As a vandal and a whore.

Gary Are you here, Judith?

Judith What?

Gary Now.

Judith I don't know, Gary.

Gary gets fully dressed, puts his jacket on and takes his keys.

Gary I'm going to get a paper.

Judith Are you angry?

Gary No. I'm tired. I'm wild tired.

He exits. Judith lies down.

SCENE NINE

The kitchen. Lily and Maud are watching the TV.

Lily Judith will see Esther tomorrow.

Maud She will.

Lily She spent fifteen pounds on a bottle of wine. Fifteen pounds. Will Esther meet her off the plane?

Maud I don't think so.

Lily Does she want him to do that or is he forcing her?

Maud I don't know. I can't hear what they're saying.

Rose walks in, very shattered.

Lily Where have you been all day?

Rose I went to the beach.

Lily John's gone. He left you a letter on your pillow.

Maud Are you all right?

Rose Great. Is Dad asleep? (*Pours herself a whiskey.*)

Lily He went out.

Rose Out?

Judith walks in.

Lily I threw my diet book on the fire.

Judith Good. That's good. Hiya.

Maud Hi. Did you stay at Gary's?

Judith I did, yeah.

Maud How was it?

Judith It was nice.

Maud So are you back on?

Judith No. No, we're not.

Maud So you still going to London, then?

Judith Yeah. Course I am.

Maud So what happened?

Judith I'm going to take some tea up to Dad.

Lily He's not there. He went to a funeral. It wasn't mine.

Judith What?

Maud I don't see how you can do that to Gary.

Judith Do what?

Maud He's waited years for you to go back to him.

Judith He's not a child.

Lily He was a child once.

Judith He's moving to London next week, anyway.

Maud Only 'cause you haven't asked him to stay. How come you got drunk with Dad anyhow?

Judith We were talking about Mum.

Maud Right.

Lily You defiled the library.

Judith I've left the doctors' appointments in the drawer. And when the gas bill comes there's a blank cheque. Just fill in the amount. All right?

Maud What?

Judith Gas bill. Cheque. Fill it in. Yes?

Maud Fine.

Judith Have you a message for Mum?

Rose Tell her I'm a slut and she's a bitch.

Lily Tell her she forgot my birthday card.

Maud I've some things for her. I put them by your bed.

Judith Post Office book is in here too.

Lily I helped Maudy wrap them. Gold tissue paper.

Maud They're next to your bed.

Judith How many things? Are they heavy to carry?

Maud Gary's waited years for you.

Judith What?

Maud Then you get together then you fuck off again.

Judith Did I ask you for your opinion?

Maud Don't talk to me like a fucking schoolteacher.

Judith Don't call me a fucking schoolteacher. What's got into you?

Maud Nothing.

Judith Just because you and Kevin are having a hard time there's no need to take it out on the rest of the world.

Maud It's got fuck-all to do with me and Kevin. Why do you twist things like that?

Judith I don't twist things. (*aware of the noise they are making*) Is John next door?

Lily He's not here. Will you stop talking about John John John now and let me listen to this?

Maud How can you listen to it with the fucking sound down?

Lily It's my telly. You be quiet.

Maud Fucking lunatic!

Judith Don't talk to Lily like that.

Maud I'll talk to her how I want to.

Judith You will not.

Maud Or what? Don't you tell me what to fucking do. You're not my mother. Nobody ever asked you to act like our fucking mother.

Rose Maud!

Judith What's this all about, Maud?

Maud What? I asked you to take something to Mum. I asked you nicely. You only have to put it in your bloody bag and you ask me how fucking heavy it is!

Judith I didn't mean anything by it.

Maud Yes you did. You can be so fucking selfish sometimes.

Rose Maud, stop it!

Maud I won't. Why are you defending her anyway? You're always saying how crap she's been to Gary?

Rose I'm not.

Judith Maudy, what is it now? Just tell us what's going on.

Maud Nothing. Fucking nothing. Fuck off and see Mum! Go! Just fucking go! And don't bother to take my fucking crap presents with you.

Patrick comes in from outside. Maud tries to control herself.

Patrick Who's pregnant? Rose?

Judith Nobody's pregnant.

Lily I'm not either.

Patrick Good. Let's have a drink to celebrate. (*He pours out some whiskeys.*) What's up, Maudy? Did Lily turn the sound down again?

Judith Maudy's fine.

Patrick I went to the shops. I bought you some tights, Judith. (*He gives her a pair of tights.*)

Judith Thanks, Dad.

Patrick I took them to the library but I couldn't see you through the window and I thought it might not be politic to call at Gary's.

Lily Where's my present?

Patrick Here. I got you stockings, Lily. (*He produces two more pairs of tights and a pair of stockings.*)

Lily Anything else?

Patrick I got you all three pairs each. Do you want them now or shall I keep them somewhere? The woman said she'd change them if they're wrong. (*He puts the bag of hosiery on the table.*)

Lily They're very nice. Do you have a fancy lady who advised you on them?

Patrick No. Why did you say that? What have you heard?

Lily I've heard nothing.

Patrick The woman in the shop helped. I'm going out on Tuesday night. Just so you know. I asked Nikki if she'd like to go out for dinner with me and so we're going to go and eat something. Together. There's postal orders here from that company for the cottage rent.

Judith Thanks, Dad.

Patrick I've split it into four. Myself and Lily are sharing a quarter. You've the rest between you.

Judith Great.

Patrick I'm going to have a bath. Does anyone mind?

Lily No. Do you know where it is?

Judith Thanks for the tights, Dad.

Patrick exits.

Rose He's sober. He hasn't had a single drink, has he?

Lily Give me my money. Let me look at it.

Maud (*in tears*) He went and bought tights for us. Everything hurts, you know?

Judith Maudy . . . Maudy . . . come here . . .

Maud Don't. Please. Just leave me alone.

Judith No. no. Listen to me. If you want to come tomorrow you just come with me. I buy another ticket and you come. It's easy.

Maud It's not easy. It's not fucking easy. She never asked me to come.

Judith She didn't ask me either.

Maud (*crying*) I want her to ask me. I don't want to gatecrash my own mother's flat. I want her to ask me how I am.

Judith (*crying*) I'm sorry, I was stupid. I'm so sorry. It's all right, Maudy. Sweetheart, it's all right.

Maud (*crying*) It's not all right. You all know her. You had more time with her. I never knew her. Not really. You say when Mum did this, when Mum did that, and I don't remember. I don't remember. Judith, I'm sorry. I'm so sorry.

Judith Maudy, it's fine, you cry, it's fine. (*taking her in her arms*)

Maud He went to the shops.

Judith (*holding her*) He did. He did. Will you come with me to London?

Maud No no. I don't want to go. Really really I don't. I'm just being stupid.

Lily Maudy. Look, Maudy. You've three hundred pounds.

Maud That's great, Lily.

Lily And I've a hundred and fifty.

Rose A date with Nikki? Fucking hell.

Maud Do you think he'll make a fool of himself?

Judith No. As long as he doesn't get too drunk.

Rose He wouldn't bring her back here, would he? I can't imagine Nikki's breasts in Dad's room.

Judith I bet he can.

Rose I bet he does.

Lily Little Nikki. I remember her running around the park naked with a bottle.

Rose Pretty much what she does now every Saturday night.

Maud What are you going to get with your money, Lily?

Lily Do you think I should save it?

Maud No. You're not allowed to. You have to spend it.

Lily Could I get . . . ? I don't know what to get. What can I get?

Maud What do you fancy? Music? Underwear? Chocolates?

Lily I'd like to buy some chocolates. But I would like to get something else too. Do I have to spend it all on one thing?

Maud No. You could get chocolates and then something else.

Lily An animal?

Maud You could get an animal but you'd have to tell us what it was.

Lily I'd like a snake, but I think it's cruel. I don't want anything in a cage. I might want a dress that's all blue and sparkling and some shoes the same and a bag and a necklace. Have I enough for that?

Judith I'm sure you do, but would you wear it, do you think?

Lily I would. Every day. Every single day. I'm going to buy you something with my money, Maud.

Maud No. I have my own. You spend it on yourself.

Lily I wanted to buy you the same dress I was going to get.

Maud No, Lily. You'd wear it better.

Lily Your mother used to sing to you when you were babies. Would you like to watch the television with the sound up?

Maud sits on the arm of Lily's chair. Lily turns the sound up.

SCENE TEN

The Pegasus. Gary and Patrick are having a pint together.

Patrick Gifford been in tonight?

Gary He's taken one of the make-up girls for an Indian.

Patrick I hope she likes the quiet type. I went to his place for the first time the other night. He doesn't possess one single book.

Gary No?

Patrick No. I said, 'What do you do if you want to read something? 'Read?' he says. 'Yes,' I say. 'What would you do?' 'Oh,' he says, 'if I feel like reading something I read that.' And there's a towel by his sink with George Street Municipal Baths written on it.

Gary He was joking.

Patrick He was fucking serious. And that's why women go for him. They think there has to be something going on beneath such a neanderthal exterior. Did you ever smoke weed, Gary?

Gary Once or twice.

Patrick Are you supposed to get visions?

Gary I don't think so. Why?

Patrick John gave me some. And it was like I was having an operation but they'd not given me enough anaesthetic. Someone was cutting my stomach open with a knife. Stuff like caviar was coming out of my belly. They were putting their hands in and fishing around for black pearls in my gut. What do you think that means?

Gary Is there anything you're worried about?

Patrick Is there anything I'm not worried about?

Gary 'Consider the end!'

Patrick What?

Gary It's the family motto.

Patrick Whose?

Gary Yours. The tribe of the Kennedys.

Patrick Fucking hell.

Rose and Maud enter.

Maud Hi, Dad. Gary.

Gary Here come the dancing girls.

Rose Hi, Gary. Patrick.

Maud How are you, Gary?

Gary Good.

Maud Have you heard from Judith at all?

Gary No. No, I've not.

Patrick Progeny. Who wants a drink?

Maud I'll get these.

Patrick No. You'll not deprive me of my pleasure.

Maud Two Bloody Marys then.

Patrick Gary?

Gary No. You're all right, thanks, Patrick.

Rose Tonight's the big night?

Patrick Let's not talk about it, eh? (*He goes to the bar.*)

Rose Look at Dad. He's like a schoolkid. He booked a table, you know. At the Locanda. There's never more than three people in there anyways.

Maud How are you, Gary?

Gary Good, yeah.

Maud You all ready for London?

Gary Not much to get ready, you know. Ticket. Bag.

Maud Have you seen Kevin in here tonight?

Gary He was with Gifford earlier.

Maud And the make-up girls?

Gary I don't know.

Maud He doesn't waste time, does he?

Gary I don't know who he was with, Maud. (*towards the bar*) You all right, John?

Maud Is that the Californian with him?

Rose Yeah.

Maud Do you think she can talk through those lips?

Gary I'll see yous all later.

Maud Stay, Gary. Please.

Gary I've some work I've got to finish. See you.

Rose 'Bye, Gary.

Maud 'Bye.

Gary exits.

Rose I might go home, actually.

Maud You will not. This is our pub. He's the fucking tourist. I'll go and say hello.

Rose No. Why would you do that?

Maud See what's going on. I'll be nice to him. Make him feel awkward. Look, look . . . her tits stay still when she moves.

Patrick comes back with the drinks. Maud goes to the bar.

Patrick Nikki's just finishing the glasses.

Rose You all right?

Patrick Why? Do I not look all right?

Rose You look great.

Patrick Not – not too dressed up?

Rose No.

Patrick You not talking to John?

Rose No.

Patrick He came and went very quickly.

Rose He did. Nikki's waving you over.

Patrick 'My master calls me. I must go.'

Patrick goes to the bar. Rose downs her drink and exits.

SCENE ELEVEN

Gary's flat. Late. Judith and Gary are sitting at his table, drinking wine together.

Judith Can I stay tonight?

Gary Should you not go home?

Judith I'm not meant to be back until Friday.

Gary Do you have no bags?

Judith I left it on the boat.

Gary Boat?

Judith I couldn't change my flight. So I got the ferry back.

Gary How was the sea?

Judith Very black.

Gary Shall I run you a bath?

Judith No. Could I possibly stay here for the week? I can't face them, Gary. Can I have a cigarette?

Gary gives her the packet. She tries to light it but can't. He lights one for her and takes hers.

Gary Stay tonight. See how you feel tomorrow.

Judith Thanks.

Gary Do you want to talk about it?

Judith You don't want me to stay till Friday?

Gary Best if you went home.

Judith You're expecting someone?

Gary Don't be ridiculous.

Judith Are you all packed for London?

Gary No. I've a few days yet.

Judith I saw her. My mum.

Gary I know. How was it?

Judith All right. Horrible.

Gary Why?

Judith She just didn't want me around, really. I got to her place the time we'd arranged and she wasn't there. So I waited in a pub across the road. She turned up an hour later. She'd had to stay late at work. We talked a bit and then I left.

Gary Where did you go?

Judith All-night caffs. She didn't ask me to stay.

Gary So what did you talk about?

Judith Not much. She put the telly on. I'd only been there about half an hour and she turned it on. I went to the toilet and burst into tears. She knew when I came back in but she didn't say anything. I told her I'd be in London a few days and she said to ring her.

Gary But you didn't?

Judith No.

Gary She was probably very nervous.

Judith Yeah. I bought her a bottle of wine. And she put it in the press. I haven't seen her in ten years and she put it away. She didn't touch me, Gary, not once.

Gary I'm sorry.

Judith Why should she touch me? Just because I wanted her to doesn't mean it was the right thing to do, does it?

Gary No.

Judith Why should she want to see me? I wasn't myself with her. My face was all fixed and my body felt stuck. My hands. I wanted her to take my hand.

Gary takes her hand.

Gary I'm sorry.

Judith She didn't look at me when we were talking. She kept looking away. I was staring at her and she kept watching the telly or the window.

Gary She probably didn't know how to handle it.

Judith Mm. She was embarrassed, Gary. My being there embarrassed her. Were you asleep?

Gary No. Are you tired?

Judith No. I'm still shaking with all the coffee I drunk.

Gary The bed's there when you want it. Pyjamas are here if you want them. (*indicates under the pillow*)

Judith Under the pillow?

Gary Yeah. Very rock'n'roll. I'll sleep on the floor.

Judith No, Gary, I want you next to me. But Gary, I don't . . .

Gary Shush.

Judith watches her hand, which is shaking.

Judith It won't stop. A woman there asked me for a cigarette.

Gary Where?

Judith In the caff. She was a junkie. Prostitute.

Gary Yeah?

Judith Yeah. She said she'd lost hers. And I just said I had none. And she was searching everywhere in a panic for her fags and I knew she wouldn't find them and that she'd ask me for money. She was crawling around under the table. In this tiny red dress with bruised legs. And then she found them. And she offered me one. She bought me a cup of coffee because I couldn't stop crying when she offered me a cigarette. I'd been so fucking mean in my head towards her, and I thought maybe that's why Mum doesn't really like me. Because I'm mean.

Gary You're not mean.

Judith I think I am. Cold. Yeah.

Gary You're not fucking cold and you're not mean and she's a stupid bitch for making you feel that way about yourself.

Judith Do you love me, Gary?

Gary I do. I'd die for you.

Judith Can we fuck?

Gary We can.

Judith Will you mind if I cry?

Gary No. No, I won't mind.

They embrace.

SCENE TWELVE

The Tiger Tandoori. Lily and John are sitting at a table drinking, having finished a huge meal. Lily is in her new blue spangly dress.

93

Lily Can I have another snake?

John (*to the waiter*) Another cobra, please. And a lassi.

Lily I always wanted a dog like Lassie. Do you like my dress, John? Can we play our game again?

John Absolutely. I love your dress. (*He empties some matches onto the table.*)

Lily I won last week. And the week before.

John You did, but I might win tonight. Okay . . . Yeats is walking along a river with Maud Gonne and they are looking at swans . . . I say, 'They stay together all their lives, you know.' . . . She says . . .

Lily (*thinks*) . . . 'They must get very fucking bored of each other.'

John Much better than the script. One point to you. Next line . . . Yeats meets Maud at a hotel and says, 'I felt that you came to me in a dream last night and that our souls came together in the strangest way.' She says . . .

Lily 'Shut up and kiss me.'

John Not sure about that one. It's been said before.

Lily It's what she would say. Give me a point. I want my point.

John It has to be an original line.

Lily I've never heard anyone in my life say it before. I made it up. Originally I have. I want a point.

John Either we play it properly or we don't play at all.

Lily Please. It's my point.

John If the next answer is brilliant you get all three points. Agreed? . . . Agreed?

Lily Tell me the next question before I agree.

John Unethical . . . but I concede . . . so . . . He's betrayed her by being with another woman. He says, 'Can you ever forgive me for looking at another when you were my Troy, my epiphany, my Byzantium?' Reply?

Lily 'Fuck off!'

John Three points to you. I think you should be writing the script, Lily . . . How is everyone at home? Patrick? Maud?

Lily Judith's still in London. Let's do first one to fifty.

John I don't think they stay open that late. Maud's meant to be here by now, isn't she?

Lily She'll be here. Let's play the game.

Rose enters.

Rose Lily. I'm to take you back.

Lily Why isn't Maud here? You said you never wanted to pick me up on my Indian Wednesdays.

Rose Kevin's ill.

John Would you like a drink?

Rose No.

John How are you?

Lily I've not finished my snake. Can I take it with me?

Rose I'll phone for a cab.

John Use my phone.

Rose I'll ask Nadeem. (*Rose exits to make the call.*)

Lily I think it's like heaven in here. Even the music.

John Do you want some fritters and cobras to take home with you?

Lily Yes, please, thank you very much. I'll save some for Judith too. Can I get her a snake as well? Do we have to finish the game there? I'm sorry that I'm old.

John You're as old as you feel.

Lily What if you feel nothing? You're sad?

John I'm stupid.

Lily No. You have intelligent hands.

John Do I?

Lily Do you what? Can I have some kulfi and pineapple fritters to take home? I love Wednesdays now, John.

John So do I, Lily.

Lily I'm going to ask Nadeem what fritters to have.

Lily gets up and exits as Rose comes back.

John Did you get one?

Rose Where's Lily?

John Ordering takeaways. Cigarette?

Rose Thanks.

John Why don't you sit down?

Rose sits.

Did you get my letter?

Rose Yes.

John Right . . . but you didn't reply?

Rose No. How's the film?

John Okay. It's quite intense, actually. I'm feeling much closer to Yeats than when I started.

Rose That's good, isn't it?

Lily returns.

Lily I've ordered fritters and a snake for Judith. Do you think they'll keep until she comes back? I thought of getting some for Esther in case she surprises us, but she won't, will she?

Rose No.

John Same time next week then, Lily?

Lily Yes, John.

John Good. Would you like to eat with us next week, Rose?

Rose I can't. I'm going out.

Lily With who?

Rose Nobody.

John The Secret Rose . . . Have you read those poems?

Rose No.

John The Rosicrucians believed that a rose bloomed on the cross when Christ died. That the crucifix was masculine and the rose feminine.

Lily And the cross married the rose?

John Something like that.

Rose There's the cab. 'Bye. (*Rose exits.*)

John 'Bye.

Lily Thank you, John, for being my hero tonight.

John It's a pleasure. Goodnight.

Lily Goodnight. (*Touches his face.*) Don't worry, John. About loss. Please. Promise?

John Loss?

Lily I will let you win next week.

Lily exits singing 'Goodnight My Love' to John, who sits and smokes

SCENE THIRTEEN

Rose's room. Rose is smoking a joint. Maud comes in.

Maud I'm sorry about tonight. I'm sorry. Kevin was really bad. I just couldn't leave him. Are you not talking to me?

Rose No.

Maud What are you smoking? Can I have some?

Rose passes the joint to Maud.

Could you not have asked them to put her in a cab?

Rose Like last time? When they took her to the beach because she said she lived there?

Maud I thought he might hurt himself. He was having an existential crisis.

Rose He wasn't having one. He is one. From birth to death. One long silent fucking scream.

Maud The state of the world disturbs him. I was a bastard to him, Rose. He was crying so I held him. Then he came to me naked. With the light on. And I didn't like his body. I didn't like the colour scheme. I probably would have liked it if I'd seen it from the start. But it just seemed like a foreign body . . . Did you speak to John?

Rose Sort of.

Maud What did you say?

Rose Nothing.

Maud He's fucked up, isn't he?

Rose We're all fucked up.

Maud Don't defend him.

Rose No. He has tried to apologise, though.

Maud They all apologise. They love it.

Rose What?

Maud Looking depressed and saying sorry for being so complicated. Implying we're simple or something. They should be trying to treat us in a way that doesn't warrant apology.

Rose You're right.

Maud He did not conduct himself with dignity and that's important in my book.

Rose Absolutely. Do you think I'm dignified?

Maud Very.

Rose Do you remember the day I went to the beach in a state? After I'd gone to John in the night?

Maud Yeah.

Rose You know the Kurdish guy who runs the tea van by the cliffs?

Maud Yeah.

Rose We fucked that day. On the floor of his van. It was pouring with rain and he offered me shelter. Do you think that's dignified?

Pause.

Maud . . . Yeah. I think that's great. That's poetry. You were rejected and you flew to a dark stranger by the sea. Besides that, he's gorgeous. I always went back for a Wagon Wheel separately from my tea and I don't even like chocolate. Plus he doesn't speak English, which is a huge added attraction.

Rose I don't even know his name.

Maud Last Tango in Ballina. It's perfect. Did anyone come to buy tea while you were doing it?

Rose No. He closed the shutter.

Maud Even more dignified, then.

Rose I don't know that most people would see it that way.

Maud We're not most people, thank fuck. So how did you actually lead up to it with no words?

Rose We smiled a bit. Gesticulated. Then I burst into tears. He was very beautiful. You know you said you didn't feel like you knew Mum?

Maud Yeah.

Rose I feel exactly the same way. But it bothers me less and less.

SCENE FOURTEEN

The kitchen. Late. Lily is by the fire. She is dressed in her new spangly blue dress and slippers. Judith walks in from outside.

Judith Hi, Lily.

Lily Hi, Lily, hi lo. You look great. Tired. You must have been partying all the time. Are they not with you? Rose and Maud went to meet you at the station.

Judith I caught an earlier train.

Lily They've been waiting ages. I've a snake for you in the fridge. And a fritter. So will you tell me everything?

Judith It was great. Mum is really well. She sends you her best.

Lily Is she working hard?

Judith She is, yeah.

Lily How was her hair?

Judith It was . . . it looked great.

Lily Long?

Judith Yeah.

Lily Good. I was worried about that. Does she have a couch and things?

Judith She does. She's got everything.

Rose and Maud come in.

Rose We were at the station. Where were you?

Judith I got in early and called in on Gary. Sorry, I didn't realise . . .

Maud How was it?

Rose How are you?

Maud How's Mum?

Judith Fine. Really good. It all went fine. She sends her best to you all. She loved your presents, Maud.

Maud Did she? What did she say?

Judith She just loved them.

Rose So what did you do? Where did you go?

Judith We stayed in and chatted most of the time. And Mum was working a lot.

Rose Did she not get time off?

Judith She couldn't, no.

Maud How is she?

Judith She's well.

Lily Did you tell her about my blue dress?

Judith I did. And she wants a photo of it.

Maud Did you take any photos?

Judith No. I forgot.

Maud I'm glad it went well. Do you feel good for seeing her?

Judith I do.

Maud I'm sorry about my being stupid. You didn't mention that to her, did you?

Judith Course I didn't. How's it all been here?

Maud Fine.

Rose Dad went on his date.

Judith My God. How did it go?

Rose They're meeting again next Tuesday.

Judith Oh my God.

Maud Tell us about Mum. From the start.

Judith Well. I got to her place and she'd cooked us a meal. And we drank wine and just talked, really.

Maud Is she going to come over soon?

Judith She's going to try, yeah.

Maud Did you go out and stuff?

Judith One night we went to a pub where they were playing music. Kilburn was great. And on the last night we went to an Italian restaurant in St John's Wood. Got completely langered.

Maud So it was brilliant?

Judith It was.

Maud I'm really happy that you had a nice time.

Pause.

Judith I came back on Sunday. I've been at Gary's all week.

Rose What? Why?

Judith I only spent an evening with Mum and it was pretty miserable. Sorry.

Lily Get your sister a drink.

Maud gives Judith a whiskey.

Rose Why would you do that? Not come home? Why did you hide?

Judith I don't know. It seemed like the thing to do.

Rose So what was all that just now?

Judith Nothing. It just came out.

Rose We were talking about you every day. What you might be doing.

Judith I'm sorry.

Rose You hid at Gary's?

Judith You always said I was never surprising.

Rose That's not surprising, that's ridiculous.

Lily Were you scared to come home, Judith?

Judith I wasn't scared. I wasn't thinking.

Rose You were thinking pretty fast just then.

Lily Be understanding to your sister.

Rose I can't be understanding if I don't fucking understand, can I?

Judith I've been an idiot.

Rose Fucking lunatic.

Lily Don't call her a lunatic. She was frightened.

Judith I've been really stupid. I'm sorry.

Rose What were you gonna do? Keep lying to us and go and visit her again next year and camp at a fucking bus stop?

Judith No. I didn't mean to lie.

Rose So what was staying at Gary's all fucking week if it wasn't lying?

Judith I don't know. I'm sorry.

Rose Fuck sorry.

Judith What do you want me to say, Rose? What do you want me to do? You tell me and I'll do it, all right? Okay?

Rose No. It's not fucking okay!

Judith So what the fuck do you want me to do?

Maud Stop it, Rose! Judith, please!

Lily Don't shout, don't shout. I want to see Esther! Where is she?

Rose She's in London where she fucking belongs!

Maud Don't, Rose, please please.

Lily I want to see her. I want to see Esther! Are you teasing me? Have you hidden her somewhere? Esther! Esther!

Judith She's not here, Lily. She's not coming here.

Lily She will! Don't you tell me what she will or won't do. Don't you tell me I'm a child or I'm a lunatic.

Maud Lily, it's all right.

Lily Everyone leaves. They've all gone. They've all gone. (*Lily puts her hands over her ears and shouts and cries.*) 'My heart is like wax . . . my heart is like wax' . . . 'I cry in the daytime but thou hearest me not; and in the night season, am not silent. I cry in the daytime but thou hearest me not and in the night season am not silent.' Make love with me, you fuckers. Make love with me! Make love with me!

Maud Lily, it's all right. We're not fighting. It's all right.

Lily I cry . . . I cry . . . I do . . . I cry . . . (*becoming more and more upset*) Make love with me! Make love with me . . . make love . . . make love with me . . . someone . . . please . . . please . . . make love with me, you fuckers! You fuckers! You fuckers!

Judith It's all right, Lily. We'll make love with you, won't we?

Rose We will, Lily . . . we will . . .

Rose holds Lily. Lily becomes abstracted and starts to look for Esther around the room.

Lily I want to see Esther! Where is she? Where's Esther? I don't want to go away! Is she hiding? Did she come back with you? Don't tease me. Please.

Judith Lily . . . she's not here . . .

Lily No. No, I see that. Yes.

Rose She never was fucking here.

Lily Don't you dare say that! Who are you anyway? Who are you? Who the fuck are you? Who are you all? Shouting and screaming . . . I'm not fucking dead, I'm not, I'm not . . .

She collapses into tears. The girls go to her and they hold each other.

I want my music. I want to hear Esther. Can I play it, please?

Rose Play what, Lily? What shall we put on?

Lily Esther. She's with her. With Kitty. Over there.

Judith No. She's alive, Lily. She's in London.

Lily She's here with Kitty. I'll play her to you.

Lily gets up and goes to Kitty's urn. From it she takes an old tape, wipes the ashes off and puts it on. She sits down with the girls. The voice is pure with a guitar. . Esther sings a few lines of Ivory Joe Hunter's 'Since I Met You Baby'.

Esther's Voice Did that sound right? Was it on? Is it on?

Patrick's Voice It's on, it's turning, look.

Esther's Voice But there's no microphone?

Patrick's Voice No, it's inside. It's that bit there. Go on.

Esther's Voice Shall I rewind it?

Patrick's Voice No, just carry on there. No one's going to hear it, are they?

Esther sings a few more bars of the song and hums to it. The girls and Lily listen.

SCENE FIFTEEN

The library. Morning. Judith is sorting through returned books. Gary enters and puts one on her pile.

Judith (*not looking up*) Thanks.

Gary Judith.

Judith Gary.

Gary Listen, I can't meet you later. I'm getting an earlier flight.

Judith I can't get cover here until two.

Gary No matter. That's why I came. To say goodbye now.

Judith Why have you changed your flight?

Gary Something came up.

Judith Who?

Gary Not someone. Something.

Judith Oh. Is this it, then?

Gary It's nice to say goodbye in here anyway. Seems appropriate. My last visit to the temple.

Judith Will you write?

Gary No.

Judith Phone me, then.

Gary You've no phone.

Judith Here. At lunchtimes.

Gary I'll see how it goes.

Judith Thank you, Gary. For last week. Everything.

Gary I'll see you.

Judith You take care.

    Gary kisses her on the cheek.

Gary Say goodbye to your family for me.

Judith Will you come back for Christmas?

Gary I doubt it. (*He walks away.*)

Judith (*shouting after him*) Gary!

Gary What?

Judith I'm pregnant.

Gary You're pregnant?

Judith No. I'm not. I just always wanted to say it in here.

Gary Right. Odd.

Judith Me?

Gary Yes. You. Anything else you'd like to shock the world with, or can I go now?

Judith You can go now.

Gary Okay. (*He starts to leave.*)

Judith Gary!

Gary Yes.

Judith I wish I was pregnant.

Gary Do you?

Judith Yes. I wish I was going to have your child.

Gary Right.

Pause.

Judith What are you thinking?

Gary I was thinking about Miss Cooper. Our old English teacher. When they locked her in the cupboard . . . Just came into my mind.

Judith Anything else?

Gary No.

Judith Right.

Gary Can you renew these books for me, Judith?

Judith I thought you didn't believe in renewals.

Gary Today's an exception.

Judith What time's your flight?

Gary No time.

Judith Good . . . Will you meet me after work?

Gary I will.

Judith I'll buy you tea.

Gary Yes. You will. I'll wait for you. Next to the graffiti. (*He leaves.*)

SCENE SIXTEEN

*The kitchen. Evening. Rose and John are sitting
drinking, dressed in black.*

Rose Is the film finished?

John They're editing it now.

Rose Will it be good?

John No. How are you?

Rose All right. I just miss her. Already. I find this the
hardest room to be in.

John Maybe you should go away for a while.

Rose I hope she wasn't lonely when she died. Or scared.

John She was very tough.

Rose No. She wasn't. She wasn't tough at all. You were
her last love. She used to come back from the Indian like
a schoolgirl.

John Why don't you come to London for a break?

Rose What would I do in London?

John Rest. Go to the park. See the pelicans.

Rose Pelicans?

John In St James's Park.

Rose I've never seen a pelican.

*Patrick, Maud, Judith and Gary enter. Judith carries
the funeral urn of Lily's ashes and places it on the table.*

Patrick (*lighting a cigarette*) It was good of you to come
over, John.

Judith She'd have been really happy to know you were here.

Gary She would. When you going back, John?

John Tomorrow.

Patrick Fucking stupid speech that priest made.

Maud It was what Lily asked for.

Patrick Doesn't make it any better, does it? The last request of a lunatic doesn't make it any more acceptable, does it?

Maud The music was nice.

Patrick They played it too quiet. Where's a fucking ashtray? Why do people come into other people's houses and tidy things away when someone dies? Why do they do that?

Judith I don't know. I didn't know who that woman was who was sweeping under the sofa. But I didn't like to ask. She was crying so hard.

Patrick With the one eye and a built-up shoe?

Judith Yeah.

Patrick That was Maureen. Lily and her were at school together. Fantastic dancer she is.

Maud I told Mum we'd ring her. Tell her how it went.

Patrick The world and his fucking wife turned up, didn't they? Nobody comes to see her while she's around but they get their best fucking dress on for a party. Who wants a drink?

Maud I'll do it, Dad.

Gary Is Nikki not coming round?

Maud She's getting the pub ready.

Patrick Yeah. She's done a nice spread. Sandwiches. Cake. If ever I go to hospital to die, don't let me lie there with all the tubes, will you? Pull them down. Burst the blood bags. Shoot me, but don't just leave me there without my tobacco. Will you?

Maud No, Dad.

Patrick And no fucking speeches. I've had enough of fucking words. I don't mind what hell is like as long as nobody tries to fucking talk to me.

Maud starts pouring drinks and gives one to Patrick. Judith takes one to Gary and sits on his knee. Patrick downs his drink. Maud refills his glass.

Gary (*raises his glass*) Lily O'Hanlon.

They raise their glasses to her.

Judith Did you talk to Kevin?

Maud Just said hello. He's going to Russia. Moscow. To visit Bakunin's grave.

Patrick He's always going to fucking Russia. He's been saying he's going to Russia for the past five fucking years. (*He raises his glass.*)

The weight of this sad time we must obey;
Speak what we feel, not what we ought to say.

He takes the lid off the funeral urn and uses it as an ashtray. Everyone watches.

What? Lily wouldn't have minded. She was a madwoman. Ashes to ashes.

He cries. Maud goes to him.

Maud Dad . . . Dad.

Patrick Put some fucking music on, hey?

Judith puts on a record. Marlene Dietrich singing 'Falling in Love Again' . . . They listen.

Maud Do you want to dance, Dad?

They get up and dance. The others watch. Judith and Gary dance too.

John Will you dance, Rose?

Rose No. Thanks.

Patrick Will you get off your ass, you miserable fucking spinster?

Rose dances with John. Coloured lights cascade and make the room into one of Lily's dream dance halls.

Blackout.

SHOREDITCH MADONNA

Shoreditch Madonna was first performed at the Soho Theatre, London, on 6 July 2005. The cast was as follows:

Martha Francesca Annis
Nick Adam Croasdell
Hodge Lee Ingleby
Devlin Leigh Lawson
Christina Alexandra Moen
Michael Daniel Rabin

Director Sean Mathias
Designer Paul Burgess
Lighting Designer Jason Taylor
Sound Designer Fergus O'Hare

Characters

Christina
in her thirties

Michael
in his thirties

Nick
in his thirties

Hodge
in his twenties

Devlin
in his fifties, Irish

Martha
in her forties

The action takes place in a derelict art space
in Shoreditch and in a bedsit in Streatham,
London, 2005.

Act One

Christina's bedsit. It is small and basic but made feminine through various scarves and découpage. A figure is under the covers. A bedside table with some objects on it including dope and tobacco.

Christina is sitting on a wooden chair, dressed in a man's pyjamas. She sings:

Christina
'There is a green hill far away
Without a city wall
Where the dear Lord was crucified,
Who died to save us all.'

The Space. A cell-like room, derelict, an old, stained mattress. Michael is setting up a video camera and lights. Nick walks in with more bags. They are setting up throughout the scene.

Michael He's late.

Nick He's always late.

Michael Sit on the mattress and I'll focus.

Nick It's wet.

Michael It's just rain.

Nick smells the mattress and puts a bin-liner over it, then sits. Michael is focusing.

Talk to me.

Nick What about?

Michael Anything. Your mouth is just a hole now. Talk.

Nick That woman phoned me. The one who came into the shop. She wants me to go round to her place tomorrow night.

Michael We need to do more of this tomorrow. What does she want you to do?

Nick She's making a short. I'd only need to be there for two hours. Fifty quid. I could get Hodge a bike.

Michael Which woman you talking about?

Nick The one with the black dress and fur coat. Yesterday. She got a couple of films out.

Michael Uh-huh. You can move now.

Nick gets up. Hodge walks in and starts to help with setting up. There are noises offstage of banging metal.

Hodge He's here.

Michael Except he's not here, is he? Else I'd be talking to him.

Hodge He says he wants a chair now. A yellow chair. He wants to do it sat down.

Michael Where is he?

Hodge Checking the locks. Seeing if they're secure.

Michael They're not going to be bloody secure if he smashes them, are they? What do you have to do for this woman?

Nick She wants to film me sitting. With my back to her. Then she wants me to walk around in her room. Just the body doing different ordinary things.

Michael Naked?

Nick No. Nothing like that.

Michael You don't think you're being a bit naive?

Nick I think it's for her degree.

Michael So is it her arse or her thesis that you're attracted to?

Nick Neither.

Michael I'd fuck her for free anyhow, wouldn't you?

Nick No.

Michael Liar.

Nick There's no connection there.

Michael That's bullshit.

Nick It's not.

Michael So tomorrow she asks you where you do your work. Next day she comes round here. She stands in front of the window. Talks about Matisse and the angles in his bodies. Smokes a cigarette. Pearl choker, little black dress. Hair up like those French schoolteachers have it.

Hodge A chignon.

Michael Exactly. Turns her back to you. Slips her dress off. Shoulderblades like Anna Karina. She's looking at you now. Naked except for a pair of silk knickers. Pigeons in the roof are vibrating. Evening sun's just catching the nape of her neck. Then she opens her mouth ever so slightly and you say, 'I'm really sorry but I've got to go and stretch my canvas.'

Nick Yeah, well, it depends.

Michael On what?

Nick We might have made a connection while she was talking about Matisse.

Michael You're a windfucker, Nick.

Nick You're an omnifucker.

Michael No. I'm very selective in my conquests. Gaffer Hodge? I've never had an aristocrat. Always thought they'd be pretty good. All that repression. The women are sort of trained, aren't they?

Hodge Trained?

Michael Finishing school. Laying the table. The emphasis is on pleasing the man, isn't it? Good wife. Good cook. They're always bending over or on their knees.

Hodge It's actually the proletariat downstairs who are on their knees.

Michael She had that smell of fucking on beige leather car seats. Leading tall silent immigrants into bedsits.

Nick Which films did she rent?

Michael Can't remember.

Hodge *Eyes Without a Face* and *Throne of Blood*.

Nick What are they about?

Michael I'm not your pimp. Watch them if you want to impress her.

Nick Who are they by?

Hodge *Throne of Blood* is Kurosawa.

Nick Samurais?

Hodge Japanese version of *Macbeth*.

Michael It's fucking terrifying.

Hodge What? The bit at the end with the arrows?

Michael No, Devlin. What happened to him is fucking terrifying.

Hodge Going to prison?

Michael No. Losing it. How does someone become mediocre when they were such a fucking genius? What the fuck's he on about a yellow chair for?

Hodge Mm. We've been talking about this project for three months and he still doesn't know my name.

Michael It's a decision, isn't it?

Hodge But why us? Why choose to work with us?

Michael The galleries won't touch him any more. He's a fucking relic, isn't he?

Hodge He knows what's going on, though. We were just talking about Badiou and inaesthetics. He knows what people are up to.

Nick He doesn't know what any of us are up to. He hasn't once asked to see our work.

Hodge He must just have a good feeling about us. He's doing it by his instincts.

Michael No. He just knows that where a group of young blokes are, girls won't be far away.

Hodge You don't like him, do you?

The sound of footsteps coming up a stone stairway.

Michael I don't know him. But he's a sly fucker. I can't decide whether he's a shark or a pussycat.

Devlin enters. He is in his fifties, physically unkempt, bohemian but not tramp-like, with various carrier bags.

Devlin Who is a pussycat?

Hodge The locks are good, aren't they, Devlin? Strong?

Devlin Nothing is strong.

Hodge No.

Devlin The walls are solid. That's good. How many pussycats could you swing in here?

Michael Twelve if they had short tails.

Devlin And sharks?

Hodge Four.

Devlin Terrifying fucking animals. They never stop swimming, do they?

Hodge No. It's biological.

Devlin Human coffins for ever on the prowl. Acoustic?

Hodge As you find it.

Devlin Then it'll do, boys, eh? I'll need a chair?

Michael We thought the mattress would be a good touch.

Devlin A chair. A yellow chair. I'll not sit on a billet with fuck stains on it.

Michael It's clean. Just old.

Devlin Is it blood?

Michael Rain.

Devlin Of a biblical shade.

Hodge I could get some sheets from my room.

Devlin No. I'll not sit on the edge of other people's mortality.

Hodge I could go downstairs and get some yellow crates from the alleyway.

Devlin If I had an affection for crates I would have been a milkman. Cowboys.

Nick What?

Michael You didn't say anything about a canary-coloured chair. We've been asking you for weeks what you might need.

Devlin I said it tonight. I told –

Hodge Hodge. Tristan Hodge.

Devlin Yes.

Michael But that was just now.

Devlin I thought the work we were doing was of a spontaneous nature?

Michael It is.

Devlin So get me a fucking chair. Now.

Michael We could get one for tomorrow.

Devlin I would like one for tonight.

Michael Let's just forget the filming, then.

Pause. Michael starts to dismantle the camera stand.

Devlin Wait. (*He opens up his wheelie-bag and produces a foldable yellow chair from it.*) It's lucky the Indians came prepared, eh, boys? Were you never in the Scouts?

Michael sets up the chair in the right place and Devlin sits on it.

Michael Okay. Let's just do a rehearsal.

Devlin readjusts himself.

Devlin I want no rehearsal. My whole life has been a fucking rehearsal.

Michael Okay. Just say a few words for level, Devlin.

Devlin I'd like to thank my mother for her exquisite indifference, my agent for perpetually pissing on me and God for creating woman.

Michael starts filming.

Michael Perfect. We're recording then.

Devlin My name is . . . No matter what my name is. Call me? Call me anytime.

Devlin laughs and strikes a good sitting pose for the camera.

SCENE THREE

Three a.m. Christina's bedsit in semi-darkness. Christina is curled up in bed with her back to us, next to 'Charlie' under the covers. She wears a black dress and pearls. She sits up on the edge of the bed in a state of insomnia. She lights a candle and starts to roll a joint.

Christina Charlie? Sorry. I can't sleep. Liam is drinking on our doorstep again. He just sits there and watches. Like a boy in a playground. He looks ten years older in the last six months. As if the alcoholic calendar is different to ours. He's only your age. You can see the blood through his skin now. He's started to walk like a boxer after a fight. Or a cowboy. Before a fight. Or a comedian who has no fight in him at all. I keep thinking that's how Jesus would be if he came back. Outcast. Sat on a step. By himself. Watching. Sorry. I'll stop talking soon. Night, Charlie.

SCENE FOUR

The Space. Devlin's recording continues. Michael films him whilst Nick and Hodge watch.

Devlin I am not a talking picture. I am a fragment like yourself. I smell rank when I am terrified. Unctuous when aroused. The hair on my chest is the texture of iron filings. I have no memory of being hairless. And no desire to return to a depilated state.

Michael Do you want to talk about your relationship to Joseph Beuys?

Devlin No. I want to talk about myself. I have caressed sirens off the edge of ships while their sisters ate away my spine.

Michael Where would you put your work in relationship to Derrida?

Devlin We are a band of hunters, gatherers. Emotional magpies, vampyrs. Cut. There is a sound, no?

Michael Pigeons. In the roof.

Devlin A child.

Nick No.

Michael No.

Hodge No.

Devlin There is the concrete sound of a child. Behind the walls.

They all listen. Rain and pigeons can be heard.

Michael No.

Nick No.

Devlin In pain.

Devlin goes to the wall and touches it. Puts his back to it and listens to it. Comes away from it.

You have the list of participants for the weekend?

Michael refers to his notebook. Hodge knows it by heart.

Hodge Yes. Anna Heartstar. Aerialist.

Devlin Good.

Hodge Brian Cafolla. Dramaturg.

Devlin Fuck.

Michael Love Harlow. Poet. Didi Amin.

Devlin Who?

Michael You worked with her before. Geraldine Jones. Welsh. She's changed her name.

Devlin Ah yes. Poor Geraldine.

Michael Ten in total. Most of them are artists.

Hodge A few of them have been hypnotised before.

Devlin We should aim for twelve. Two more. Women.

Hodge Why women?

Devlin Because they smell sweeter. We can light the fires?

Hodge Yeah. We've got wood from the skips. Chopped. Downstairs.

Devlin Feels like a house in the forest. Leave me now, boys. I want to listen.

Michael We should get some more down on tape.

Devlin Should we? I am a man, not a machine. You could buy a dozen bottles of claret if you want to be useful. Doesn't have to be expensive. I know you're not the White Cube. Nor would ever want to be, eh, boys? This is a good space. It is very present. I'll join you downstairs in a while. I'll need some petty cash later. For research purposes. Leave the camera if you would, please.

Hodge Watch out for the stairs. They're slippery with the rain. It's the pigeons.

Devlin I'd rather have pigeon shit on the stairs than elephant shite on the walls. Don't worry about me. I have a good nose for excrement.

Hodge, Michael and Nick leave. Devlin produces a small bottle of vodka from his coat and a glass. He pours a drink and raises it to the walls.

Are you there? Of course you're there. You're always fucking there.

SCENE FIVE

Christina's bedsit. She turns on a lamp which gives a little light and sits back on the bed next to 'Charlie', who is under the covers. She drinks water.

Christina It still smells like school in the bathroom. Like TCP. I tried to take those mirrors off but they're fixed. If I lie down will you touch my back with your hand? Your hand feels bigger than my ribcage some nights. Will you

trace my dinosaur-skeleton spine with your nicotine
fingers? Please? Please. Thank you. How's your leg?
Thank you. For being so kind.

She lies down next to 'Charlie'.

SCENE SIX

*Devlin is recording himself. He is very drunk by now.
His face might be relayed huge and iconic on a
backcloth.*

Devlin I have been severed from the art world like a
dismembered limb. Skin still fluttering like pink ribbons
as the leg is torn from the hip socket. I no more want a
retrospective than a testicular tumour or thrombosis.
I have as little desire to show my work as my genitals.
I am not the long-lost twin of the loitering flasher who
displays his hanging puzzled scrotum from behind his
tired trench coat. I have been living in the shadows.
Chiaroscuro. Where the light is kinder. I have forgotten
the texture of early morning light. I hope to retreat from
this space changed. Dignified. Ashamed. Beheavened.
Cut. I can hear you. Come out, come out, wherever you
are. I'll count to ten. One . . . two . . . three . . . four . . .

SCENE SEVEN

*Outside the Space. There are some yellow crates. Martha
is sitting on one of them. She has an A to Z in one hand.
With her other hand she is feeling her heartbeat. Hodge
comes out of the shadows and shocks her.*

Martha Jesus!

Hodge Sorry. Sorry. I didn't mean to scare you.

Martha You made me jump.

Hodge Are you alright? Are you looking for somewhere?

Martha No, I'm fine.

Hodge Oh, right. I just came down for something that's
. . . It's actually underneath where you're sitting.

Martha gets up.

Hodge Sorry. I didn't mean to disturb you. Are you
looking for the art space?

Martha Yes. Are you part of it?

Hodge I am, yeah.

Martha Oh. Right. I need to speak to Devlin. The
painter. I wanted to do the weekend forum. He's taking
it, isn't he? Do you know him? Is he there?

Hodge Yeah, he's upstairs. I wouldn't call it a forum,
though, else he'll start shouting. I'll take you up to him.

Martha No. Actually. I'll come back.

Hodge He's not in the middle of anything.

Martha No. I'll come by tomorrow. Are you alright?

Hodge Yeah.

Martha Just you seem terribly nervous.

Hodge No. I'm always like this. I prefer to think of it as
being alert.

Martha To what?

Hodge Potential hazards. You know. Men at bus stops.
Moths in my room. Women.

Martha Women doing what?

Hodge Anything, really. Shall I give him a message?

Martha Tell him a ghost came by to see him.

Hodge Okay. (*He starts to go.*) You should be careful round here. This time of night it can get a bit . . .

Martha A bit what?

Hodge . . . heated.

Hodge starts to go but Martha remains seated.

Are you waiting for someone?

Martha We're all waiting for someone, aren't we?

Hodge nods and leaves.

SCENE EIGHT

The Space. Devlin is drunk.

Devlin One hundred and sixty-five, one hundred and sixty-six , one hundred and sixty-seven, sixty-nine, sixty-nine . . . fuck . . . one thousand and one, one thousand and two. Nights, days, fuck it . . . There's a clock in the bar around the corner. Big fucking megalithic thing and it shows how many seconds are left before closing time. Counts them down. Very fucking loud it is. You might like it. Will I show it to you? Are you coming out or not?

He folds into himself.

SCENE NINE

Christina's bedsit. Christina gets up off the bed leaving 'Charlie' asleep. She is in a state of sleepwalking.

Christina Charlie. Charlie. You've got to get up now. It's time to get up. You have to get your train to Liverpool, sweetheart. Your appointment's at eleven. Charlie. Charlie, come on. You can't miss it. They'll fuck you around even more if you don't get there. Charlie.

She pulls back the covers and reveals 'Charlie', who is simply pillows. She takes down the pillows and lies with them on the floor as if they were a person.

SCENE TEN

The Space. Martha is waiting. She is looking through a large coffee-table art book on Devlin's work. Michael comes in with two takeaway teas.

Michael Sorry. I had to go outside for them. And there was a queue. Hodge had locked his room.

Martha What?

Michael The kettle. Mugs. They're in Hodge's room.

He gives her a tea.

Martha Oh. Thanks. That's great. I didn't even know this book existed.

Michael Yeah. Devlin's very big in Germany. Sugar?

Martha Thanks.

He gives her a little cafe packet of sugar.

Got a . . .?

Michael Spoon. No. Pen?

Martha No, you're fine. It's a huge space. You've made it beautiful downstairs.

Michael Yeah. We do the big shows down there. Smaller events up here.

Martha Is it just your own work?

Michael No no. We've had about thirty shows since we've been here. All different artists.

Hodge comes in carrying a shop mannequin.

Hodge It's you.

Michael Hodge, this is Martha. She's going to do the weekend forum. What did you lock your room for?

Hodge No reason. Martha.

Michael You two know each other?

Martha No, we've never met before.

Hodge No? No.

Martha Who's your friend?

Hodge That's a big question, isn't it?

Michael Hodge rescues things. We've had cats, dogs, drunks. We rehoused a crow here last Christmas, didn't we?

Hodge Oh yes. Rip. Till his wing got better.

Michael We were making a film on Dartmoor last summer and we found Hodge trying to put a sheep in the van.

Hodge Yeah, I thought it was lost. Or abandoned.

Michael Do you know Devlin?

Martha I do. I went straight from a convent school to his teaching me at St Martin's. I was the only one who used to blush in life drawing.

Hodge You were touched by nuns? Sorry. Taught by nuns?

Martha Taught and touched. I was a lamb to the slaughter. Is she going to be part of your work?

Hodge What? I'm doing a project on control versus spontaneity. I thought I might use this as a map of human . . . something. What do you think of Devlin's work?

Martha He was amazing. Then he got scared.

Devlin enters. He is carrying various newspapers.

Devlin Who is scared?

Martha You, Devlin. You must be fucking terrified.

Devlin Is it you?

Martha You're thinner.

Devlin You're older.

Martha Yeah. Thank God.

Devlin Leave us alone together, would you, boys? Please. Please?

Hodge Tristan and Michael.

Devlin Yes, of course. Tristan. Mickey. Go and look for Iseult and Minnie. They're out there somewhere. It's only a question of time, your locating them.

Michael See you again, Martha.

Martha I hope so. Goodbye, Hodge.

Hodge Yes.

Hodge and Michael leave. Devlin goes to Martha. He touches her face. He puts his hand gently around her neck.

Devlin Marta. Marta. God. I trust my senses less and less these days. But it's you.

Martha It is.

Devlin Twelve years, is it? Christ. And you found me here in Fagin's den with the Fournier Street Irregulars. That's incredible. I've been living in Bulgaria.

Martha I know.

Devlin Did you imagine I'd been devoured by wolves?

Martha No. I thought you'd make friends with them.

Devlin I did. I felt very at home with the extraordinary sounds they made at night. I'm sure we'd all be healthier and happier if we were permitted to howl at the moon like they do without an ASBO being issued by the neighbours next door. It's a fantastically beautiful country, Marta. The forests.

Martha I know. I went there. For a holiday.

Devlin You did? When were you there?

Martha About six years ago.

Devlin You should have looked me up.

Martha You didn't leave a forwarding address. Are you going back?

Devlin No. I had a dalliance out there with the wife of a local mafia man. My choice was London or a meat hook. I was quietly surprised at my suddenly profound desire to stay alive and experience more of the same repetitions. It's good to see you, Marta.

Martha I've put my name down for your weekend.

Devlin No. No, you mustn't do that.

Martha Why not?

Devlin It's boredom on a plinth.

Martha They all seem excited about it.

Devlin Those boys would get excited over a dog pissing against a tree. Why are you here?

Martha I heard about Charlie.

Devlin I thought that must be it.

Martha It suddenly felt important to forgive you.

Devlin Thank you. I've no idea what for, but thank you. Are you still painting?

Martha No. I found it too flat. It reminded me of you. Why did Charlie do it?

Devlin Drugs. He was injecting three times a day. I think he was simply tired. Very tired. (*Pause.*) It's always awkward how much time one allots to the dead, isn't it? Are you seeing someone?

Martha Yeah. He's twenty-seven.

Devlin A boy-child. Wonderful. I'm impotent now, you know.

Martha My God. Is that a blessing or a curse?

Devlin It depends whose side you're on. Actually it's somewhat of a release.

Martha So how do you find your way around without your cock?

Devlin I had to buy an *A to Z*.

Martha I wrote you so many letters.

Devlin You did.

Martha I thought you'd be lonely in prison.

Devlin I was.

Martha No. You're never lonely.

Devlin I'm always lonely, Marta. Don't rob me of my artist's badge. What you mean is I'm rarely alone. Your letters were received with open arms. But you can't fuck an envelope.

Martha So who did you fuck?

Devlin A couple of the boys there. One was the spitting image of Donatello's David. Mouth like a sewer. The contrast beguiled me.

Martha What happened to the girl you went inside for?

Devlin No idea. But less of the girl. She was fifteen. Perhaps she became a solicitor. How is your work?

Martha Good. I'm working on a series of sculptures about mirror images.

Devlin Metal?

Martha Wood. I'm using a lot of found objects.

Devlin And you're making a decent living? That's fantastic.

Martha Don't you want to know what they're about?

Devlin We'd probably need a week, wouldn't we? But someone's buying them?

Martha There's a gallery which sells them. 'Skin Four'.

Devlin The one under the arches?

Martha Yes.

Devlin Tsk tsk, Marta.

Martha What?

Devlin Come on. I met them at one of their openings. Couldn't see the paintings for all the fucking sushi and asahi.

Martha Nothing wrong with throwing a good party. You went to it.

Devlin Only because the booze was gratis. Pseuds fucking corner, isn't it? Just their names. Illy. Miko. Kat. They sound like a Japanese boy band and they all hail from Willesden fucking Junction. How much of a cut do they take?

Martha Fifty per cent.

Devlin Thieving little office-boy pricks. All they can do is pixellate. Christ, London's gone to the dogs. Where are you living?

Martha Bayswater.

Devlin We used to visit the cafés along there. I'd smoke a hookah and we'd read Rumi's poems together.

Martha That wasn't me. That was someone else.

Devlin Ah. Well, it should have been you. You haven't found religion, have you, Marta?

Martha No.

Devlin What have you found?

Martha looks at some sketches around the room.

Martha You. I've found you.

She looks at him.

Devlin You have. This is perfect. I'll go and get a few bottles in and we'll have a proper old restoration gossip, shall we? I actually gave the last of my funds . . . to the boys. They struggle, you know, with the space and all.

I mean, if you provide for tonight I'll do the honours next time. Tomorrow. Whenever.

Martha gives him some money. He touches her neck as if drawing her.

Don't move! I used to say that for effect to you. But I mean it now. Stay. Yes?

Martha I'll stay. At least until you get back.

He kisses her cheek and rushes out. Martha sits.

SCENE ELEVEN

Christina's bedsit. Christina is checking her appearance and now puts a black scarf over the mirror to cover it. The bell rings. She presses an intercom buzzer and opens the door a little. She puts Bach on the tape recorder. Nick knocks at the open door.

Christina Hi. Thanks so much. For coming round.

Nick Hi. Nick.

Christina Great. Come in. Sit down.

Nick Thanks.

He sits. She switches off the music.

Christina Drink?

Nick Lovely.

Christina What would you like?

Nick You got some white wine?

Christina No. No. I have Pilsener? Or lemonade?

Nick Pilsener. Great.

Christina Do you want a glass or is a tin okay?

Nick Tin's good. So you're making a short film? What's it about?

Christina I prefer not to talk about my work, if that's okay.

Nick Fine. I'm the same.

Christina You don't like talking about the video shop?

Nick We're all temporary at Solaris. The wages go into an art space that we run.

Christina Yes, I know. We have a mutual friend. Devlin.

Nick Uh-huh. Yeah, he's doing some work with us at the moment.

Christina I don't really know him. We only met the once. He's a friend of a friend. What's he like?

Nick He's the last of the bohemians.

Christina Is he? Here's to them.

> *She gives him a beer and puts a glass ice bucket next to him.*

Nick Cheers. (*He picks up a video from the table.*) *Throne of Blood.* Brilliant. Best filming of Shakespeare I've seen. Fantastic.

Christina It's not Shakespeare though, is it?

Nick Isn't it?

Christina The language is so sparse.

Nick Yeah.

Christina I like the arrows at the end.

Nick Yeah, they're amazing.

Christina What did it make you think of?

Nick The arrows? . . . Death.

Christina They always made me think of a hedgehog.

Nick Yeah? Yeah, I can see that. Do you share with someone?

Christina What?

Nick Nothing. Can I smoke in here?

Christina No. I mean yes. I thought you were minding if I, asking if I minded.

Nick Do you have an ashtray?

Christina I must have one. I do. I know I do.

Nick I've found one.

Christina Good.

Nick offers Christina a cigarette but she shakes her head. He lights up and they both sit down.

Can I ask you something? Hypothetically? How much would you charge to stay with someone for the night?

Nick What?

Christina It's the exchange of money for bodies. It fascinates me.

Nick I'd only stay with someone because I wanted to.

Christina Absolutely. But there's something rather wonderful about money on a bedside table, don't you think? I never married anyone.

Nick No?

Christina No. My hands are clean. (*She puts her hands into the ice bucket.*) It's good for the circulation. Geisha girls had to do this for hours. They started to bind girls' feet when they were six years old. A little mound of cracked child bones that they could only hobble around on like a broken doll. Men can be very brutal, can't they?

Nick They can.

Christina Don't take any notice of me if I say something awol. I took a shitload of drugs last week.

Nick That's brilliant. That's fantastic. What did you take?

Christina I tried to kill myself.

Nick Oh.

Christina Sorry. Has my suicide status unnerved you?

Nick No. No, it hasn't.

Christina The film's about a man in a green jumper. Faceless. I'll talk you through it later.

Nick Right. (*Pause.*) Why did you do it?

Christina Why? I didn't do it, did I? It's statistical, actually. I was reading about it. Men tend to do the deed whereas women are often crying out for help. The Americans have got this new prescription for depression. For people who live by themselves. They're told to put a video next to their bed and when they wake up they're supposed to switch it on and watch the person on screen for an hour before getting up. I was missing someone.

Nick Who are they watching?

Christina Anyone. As long as they're talking. About anything. It's supposed to form an impression of company. What do you think?

Nick It's the loneliest thing I ever heard of.

Christina Yes. But if it was the right tape?

Nick Do you have friends? Family in London?

Christina No. I've only got Charlie.

Nick Charlie?

Christina Yes. But he's dead. Yes. Charlie's dead.

Nick I'm sorry.

Christina Why? You didn't kill him, did you?

Nick No.

Christina No. No, he 'killed himself'. Three weeks ago today. Morning is the most popular time for it. And spring is the most favoured month. I suppose that if you feel that removed, it must just seem unbearable to watch things grow, mustn't it?

Nick Yeah.

Christina There's an apple blossom tree next to the bathroom window. And when I found him . . . do you mind me talking about this?

Nick No. Of course not.

Christina I came home and everything was switched on. The television. Sound down. The iron. All the lights. Radio. Anything electrical. I was planning to use the film we make to wake up with in the morning. Would you mind if I did that?

Nick No. No, I don't mind.

Christina Thank you. Do you mind? Really? Because I could ask somebody else. There's this man, Liam, who often sits on our step and I'm sure he'd do it.

Nick You didn't tell me about the tree. Outside the bathroom.

Christina Oh. Yes. It was just that petals from the blossom had flown in through the window and they were all over the floor and in the bathtub. Like confetti. It looked like a couple had stood in the bath and had been married there. Except they hadn't. He was hanging there with these petals under his feet.

Nick I could stay. Tonight. On the floor. If that would help you.

Christina Why would you do that?

Nick Why not?

Christina Won't someone miss you if you don't return?

Nick Possibly. I'll text her. Tell her that I'm playing poker.

Christina Do you lie to her?

Nick Sometimes.

Christina Why?

Nick Because women are so beautiful. I'll need to get some more cigarettes.

Christina Take the keys. Don't ring. Just come in. But put a scarf on. It's cold out there.

Nick I'm fine.

Christina Please. You might get ill. And if you borrow the scarf you have to come back.

Nick What's your name?

Christina Christina. Please. For me. Wear this. For protection.

She puts a woolly scarf around his neck and knots it in a familiar way.

SCENE TWELVE

The Space. Devlin and Martha are finishing a second bottle of wine. They are both a bit drunk.

Devlin Can I see your legs?

Martha Fuck off.

Devlin You've not become a prude, Marta?

Martha I'm not showing you my fucking legs.

Devlin I want to see if they've changed. Mine are repulsive now. Arterial. Varicose. Like a view from an aeroplane. And I'm losing my memory. It worries me. When I remember to worry about it. Do you remember things?

Martha Yeah. Every freckle on your shoulder.

Devlin Repulsive things.

Martha You always were a physical fascist.

Devlin Ruskin disowned his own wife for less.

Martha Do you remember our first date? You pulled me into that black cab?

Devlin No.

Martha Yes you do. You held my hand tight against your velvet trousers and you had a huge erection.

Devlin Halcyon days.

Martha I thought it was cancer. I burst into tears 'cos I thought you liked me enough to tell me you were terminally ill.

Devlin You look beautiful, by the way.

Martha Who found Charlie?

Devlin Fuck . . . His girlfriend. He hung himself from a pipe in the bathroom.

Martha Shit. I keep seeing him as a little boy since I heard about it.

Devlin He didn't leave a note. Just my name and number on a Rizla paper in his pocket. His girlfriend rang me. I sat on the edge of the bath staring at him. I've never seen a hanged man, Marta. He looked like a cartoon. Like the printing had fucked up with the lines and colours. His forearms were a deep dark red and his chin too. I was fascinated by this discolouration. I asked the sergeant about it. He said the blood had pooled. Pooled. It sounds so gentle, doesn't it? I harangued him when I saw him last. I was not kind to him.

Martha You were always good with him.

Devlin When he was a child. It was always a pleasure dragging him away from that fucking children's home. But when he became the confusion that was his adult life, I was impatient.

Martha You were his hero.

Devlin I didn't ask to be his fucking hero. Why did he write my name down, Marta? You've taken to wearing trousers? That's unfair.

Martha What?

Devlin You should give people permission to dream.

Martha Your whole life revolves around sex, doesn't it?

Devlin It has to. It's primal, isn't it? Every artistic expression is an instinct to procreate. Works of art should bear one universal title: 'Fuck me, please.' They could print it in Latin if it offended.

Martha Could it not read 'Love me, please'?

Devlin Loving. Fucking. It's the same thing. Everyone I have fucked I have loved, Marta. For a moment. Or a minute. Or a month. I think my problem is only temporary. I'm reading a book about it. They keep talking about men in their caves, don't they? What they omit to mention is that some of the most beautiful paintings existent are at Lascaux.

Martha It used to make me cry, all those fucking manuals you read. Sex. Psychology. Female sensibility. You had one for everything, didn't you?

Devlin Except one for living. That one escaped me.

Martha You were impotent for a while when we were together.

Devlin No. Not so. I was intimidated by your affair with that African prince. Affected, not impotent. My last foray has changed her name to Didi Amin. Are people born that lost?

Martha Can you be reliable, Devlin?

Devlin God no. But if I can help. You know how discreet I am.

Martha You were the biggest bloody gossip of them all.

Devlin Possibly. But all our circle is dead now or in Wales so there's only the sheep to tell it to. So do you fancy a fuck for old times' sake?

Martha No. I really don't.

Devlin It was a joke. I told you I'm flaccid as a cherub these days.

Martha Why did you give up painting?

Devlin Brando is dead. Did you know? Can I take your hand?

She gives him her hand.

That's sweet. Very sweet. (*He smells it.*) Like all the perfumes of Arabia.

He sits down with her hand in his.

Will you put your hand on my head?

She puts it on his brow. He takes a couple of breaths then moves her hand to his groin.

Martha We lived a lot, didn't we?

Devlin We did. We did. Your hands were always so pale. Like Rodin's Cathedral.

Martha takes her hand away from his groin.

Martha What's happened to you, Devlin?

Devlin What's happened to us all?

Martha Seriously.

Devlin The lights go out, don't they? No more cerebral activity. No thinking allowed. Would you hold me, Marta?

She holds him in her arms.

Can I put my head in your lap? Listen to your stomach, like the old days? (*He moves into this position.*) I can hear your womb. Like the Red Sea. I can't paint any more, Marta. It's a very particular sensation. Like living with a stranger who is lodged inside my skin.

Martha Your pictures used to make my heart stop, Devlin. I'd look at them and cry, they were so honest.

Devlin I can't make sense of anything, Marta.

Martha How long was it before you could make sense of things after Hildy died?

Devlin separates himself from Martha.

Devlin Perhaps you should go.

Martha You never talked about it to anyone.

Devlin Fuck off. She died. She was my child. Her bones had not even become themselves. What more is there to say?

Martha Nothing. I should go.

Devlin No. Marta. Please. We're not fighting are we? Come here my compadre. My Shoreditch Madonna.

Martha You come here, Devlin.

Devlin I will. I've been invited. I don't know why mountains and Mohammed had such issues with movement.

He goes to Martha and puts his arms gently around her. She puts her arms around him. He kisses her gently.

Marta. You still smell of oranges, Marta.

He holds her very tight.

My Gio-fucking-conda. Anaconda gioconda.

He loses himself in her and now starts to kiss her and tries to undress her.

Marta. Sweet Marta. Will you be my mother, Marta?

He puts his mouth to her breast.

Sweet Marta. Are you my mother?

Martha pushes him off.

Martha Fuck off, Devlin! I'm not your fucking mother.

Devlin I wasn't for a moment implying you were. It was a metaphor, Marta. An invocation of the sexual matriarch.

Martha You're not even impotent, are you? It's just another line.

Devlin That's as much as you know. But I don't blame you. I did you a lot of damage.

Martha I did damage to myself. You had nothing to do with it.

Devlin I'm sorry my touching you was upsetting. I thought you might have changed.

Martha You're a cold bastard, Devlin.

Devlin I am. But I have no choice but to live a life consigned to me. Whereas you have chosen to spend a great deal of your adult existence chasing me. What does that say about you, Marta?

Martha I was in love with you. Love's a fever. And incredibly indiscriminate. And I wasn't fucking chasing you.

Devlin Quite so. Mea culpa. It's good that you're angry. Good to let it all out.

Martha Fuck off, Devlin. Why do you always make me feel like a patient? You've always been so fucking formulaic. Woman angry, antidote A. Woman aroused, antidote B.

Devlin Me? Formulaic? I've never been formulaic. But are you? Aroused?

Martha No. Most definitely absolutely not.

Devlin So what's next? Do you want to berate me for the crushing oppression of your childhood to which I was not in fact party?

Martha I never fucking chased you.

Devlin I never asked you to write to me in prison, Marta. You bleated of your own accord.

Martha Do people seriously pay money to spend a weekend with you? Because you used to go to piss-ups with artists who make them salivate? Christ, you're so full of shit.

Devlin You could probably go now. If you wanted to.

Martha I am going. I used to watch you paint. You were so fucking brilliant, Devlin. I went to see your show at Venice last year. I felt embarrassed for you. It didn't resemble anything connected to real emotion. It felt more like you were trying to piss and it was painful. It was arthritic. Like the brushes were strapped to your wrists with barbed wire. Felt less like painting than pissing blood and ice.

Martha exits. Devlin puts his head in his hands.

SCENE THIRTEEN

The Space. Nick is playing a drum. He is lost in the music and his thoughts. He is very much on his own.

SCENE FOURTEEN

Christina is in her bedsit. She is playing the film of Nick's back onto her body. She is wearing underwear so that the film projects onto her body and she moves with it. Nick might lie down in the film and Christina might lie down with him and 'hold' him.

Christina Charlie. How are you? There was another
man here. In your space. I thought it might make you
come back for me. If I bent over for him would you kick
the door down? Hit him? Crush his head until he didn't
exist. Would you kiss my neck, Charlie? My eyes? We
wasted so much time, didn't we? I hate other people,
Charlie. I hate anyone who doesn't want to wash your
feet. I hate them. I won't stay here. It doesn't make
sense. Any of it. I'll see you soon. Be with you. Soon.
Love's fantastic, isn't it?

SCENE FIFTEEN

*The Space. Hodge is talking to the mannequin whilst
painting it. The dummy is on a plastic platform so that
with his foot he can imperceptibly make her lean
forward and back.*

Hodge She smells like oranges. Did you notice that? Her
skin is translucent. And the shape that her breasts made
under her shirt. She's like the Venus de Milo. Plus arms.
She looked very lost with her book of streets. I wish
she'd get ill so I could look after her. Not very ill. Just a
cold. Blanket. Lemsip. Copies of *Viz*. Or maybe *Vogue*.

SCENE SIXTEEN

*The Space. There is a 'Teach Yourself Arabic' tape
playing and Michael is repeating the phrases.*

Tape Yes. *NaAhm.*

Michael *NaAhm.*

Tape No. *Laa.*

Michael *Laa.*

Tape Please point to the phrase in the book. *Ashir ilaal Ahibaara feel kitaab, lau samaHt.*

Michael *Ashir ilaal Ahibaara feel kitaab, lau samaHt.*

Nick enters.

Nick What you listening to?

Michael Arabic. The language of love.

Nick You're not going away, are you?

Michael Not if it involves going anywhere with myself, no.

He turns off the tape.

Nick You okay?

Michael Yeah. You?

Nick Yeah.

Michael How did it go with that woman?

Nick Okay. How's Devlin?

Michael I've got the feeling he's going to bolt.

Nick Why?

Michael Maybe it's just me. I feel like everything's going away.

Nick Right.

Michael We've been lucky for three years. Invisible. Could get moved on any time now.

Nick Yeah. We've always known that.

Michael What would we do? Find somewhere else around here?

Nick Maybe. There's the old brewery. Loads of room for us and Hodge.

Michael Yeah. But Hodge'll probably want to move south if he gets that teaching job.

Nick I stayed the night on her floor.

Michael Did you?

Nick Yeah. I don't think she slept. She was breathing heavily and moving around. I stayed awake all night listening. And then I kept imagining waking up next to her. Seeing her head on the pillow next to me.

Michael Decapitated?

Nick Piss off. You got any dope?

Michael Leather jacket next to my bed.

Nick Can I take some? I said I'd go round there tonight. It might help her to sleep.

Michael You shouldn't go round there again tonight. It's too keen.

Nick Her boyfriend just hung himself. It's not the time to be playing games, is it?

Michael Probably not the appropriate time to be trying to fuck her either.

Nick That's not what I'm going there for.

Michael Right. My mistake. I'm thinking of leaving the Space.

Nick What? Why?

Michael I just think it might be time to do something on my own.

Nick Why?

Michael Why not?

Nick Because we've been leading up to a big exhibition for the past three years.

Michael We can still do that.

Nick A minute ago you were saying we'd go to the brewery.

Michael I've gone off the idea.

Nick What?

Michael I want to have more time to paint. I didn't start this whole thing just to answer fucking emails.

Nick Me and Hodge are always offering to do it.

Michael It's not as simple as that, is it? You get into a dialogue with people. You can't suddenly say, oh, my mate's taking over now. I'm the only one who knows what's going on with everyone.

Nick Because you won't let us touch it.

Michael Yeah. Probably. Possibly.

Nick You're not really thinking of leaving, are you?

Michael No. Not really.

Nick You okay?

Michael Yeah. Cabin fever. I'd better check on Devlin. Good luck with the merry widow.

Michael leaves.

SCENE SEVENTEEN

Christina's bedsit. Nick is lying on the floor. Christina is in bed. She seems to wake up. Her eyes are open but she

*is sleepwalking. She goes over to Nick and touches him
gently.*

Christina Hey. Did we fight?

Nick Mm? What? No.

Christina Why are you sleeping here?

Nick You asked me to stay again. Do you remember?

Christina No. Sorry. Was I horrible?

Nick No.

Christina I didn't mean it.

Nick What?

Christina Whatever I said. Sweetheart. Is your leg okay?

Nick Yeah, it's fine.

Christina You took your pills for it?

Nick What?

Christina Let me see your leg, Charlie.

Nick I'm not . . .

*Christina pulls back the blanket and looks at Nick's
leg. She touches it gently. Kisses it.*

Christina Come to bed.

Nick To bed?

Christina Yeah. Please.

She strokes his hair and his face and kisses his face.

Is that nice?

Nick It's lovely.

She takes off her shirt and puts his hand on her breast.

Christina That's yours.

Nick Yeah?

She moves his hand to different parts of her body.

Christina And that. And that. And this. It's yours.

Nick Christina . . .

Christina I remember us fucking right here. I had bruises on my arms because you held me so tight. Beautiful sea-green imprints of your fingers on my skin. Do you remember? Fucking me here? Very slowly. Then very hard.

Nick does not reply.

Do you remember Charlie? Do you?

She kisses him.

Nick Yeah. Yeah, I remember.

Christina Come to bed. We never fuck any more. Come to bed and fuck me. Please. Please.

Nick Okay.

Christina How? How will you fuck me?

Nick Very slowly. Then very hard.

Christina Yes, Charlie. Very slowly. Then very hard.

She takes his hand and leads him into bed. They get into bed. Touch each other gently.

Lights down.

Act Two

Christina's bedsit. Christina is lying down on her bed like a rag doll, splayed. Devlin is sitting on the floor. He reaches for his vodka in his coat. He is exhausted. Christina is as if drugged and in a semi-trance state under hypnosis. She sings.

Christina
'We may not know we cannot tell
What pains he had to bear,
But we believe it was for us
He hung and suffered there.'

She hums the tune.

Devlin Christina. Chrissy? Do you want a drink? Have a drink, will you?

Christina gathers the covers around her. She comes to, sitting with a huge effort.

Christina Do I have to give it back to you? From my mouth?

Devlin You've gone under very deep, Christina. How are you feeling?

Christina Worried.

Devlin What's worrying you?

Christina Charlie's leg. It's putrid. It smells, but I don't want him to know that. If he was a soldier he'd be a hero, wouldn't he?

161

Devlin He would. Did he ever talk about me, Christina? About Devlin?

Christina He said that you were hiding from him. In a red room in Austria.

Devlin I want you to try and picture him. Can you see him now?

Christina Yes. He's surrounded by metal and they're shaving his hair. They're cutting off his toenails and they're writing on his body. His beautiful body. He looks thinner.

Devlin What are they writing?

Christina Words.

Devlin Can you read them?

Christina Gitane, tsigane, gypsy. They're letting his blood and writing that with it.

Devlin Are you with him?

Christina No. They've made me stay on a plastic chair. And I'm not allowed to stand up.

Devlin Have they tied you up?

Christina No. But I'm not allowed. And I'm wet. I've pissed myself. And my thighs are beginning to rub. I've got my hand up but they're not taking any notice of me.

Devlin Is he angry with us, Christina?

Christina He's fucking furious.

Devlin Why?

Christina Because we lied to him.

Devlin Both of us?

Christina Everyone. But especially me. And most of all you.

Devlin What did I lie about?

Christina You said you loved him, but you were lying.

Devlin Can you talk to him?

Christina No.

Devlin Why not?

Christina Because he's dead. Is why. Because he's dead. He be. He be. He do the police in funny voices. He be dead.

She starts to get upset.

Devlin I want you to lie back down and I'm going to bring you out of it.

Christina No. I want to stay with him.

Devlin I'm just going to bring you back gently.

Christina You can't make me. No one can.

Devlin Charlie doesn't want you to stay there.

Christina Fuck off. You're a liar, Devlin. You can't see inside his head. I'm staying where I can see him.

Devlin The state is temporary. Do you understand?

Christina Everything. Everything.

Devlin lights a cigarette.

They're cutting you up into tiny pieces, Charlie. Because you never fitted in they're trying to make a human jigsaw out of your flesh and make it fit this time. They're slicing you up like a dog off the streets. They're drawing plans to burn your skin and pull your teeth out. Because you wouldn't do what they told you to do. Because you wouldn't fill in the forms.

Devlin leans over her and puts his hand on her forehead. He closes her eyes. He kisses her brow. He whispers into her ear. She wakes as from a very deep sleep.

Devlin Are you alright?

Christina Mm.

Devlin You want a drink? Some water?

Christina No.

Devlin You were out for a long time. Do you remember what you saw?

Christina Charlie. He was lying down.

Devlin Nothing else?

Christina No. Was there something else?

Devlin No. No, there was nothing else.

SCENE TWO

The Space. Martha, Michael and Nick are sharing a bottle of wine. Martha and Michael are completely drunk and stoned. Nick is not. Hodge is drawing lines on the lower body of the mannequin.

Nick Do you think he meant it?

Hodge Who?

Nick Devlin. He said that it would be healing for her.

Michael No. He's probably filming her now. He's clicked his fingers and told her to start dancing round in her baby doll nightie.

Nick Stop it.

Michael It was a joke, Nick.

Nick You've got a sick sense of humour.

Michael No. I've just got an incredibly vivid imagination. And if I didn't possess one we never would have moved into this building and created an empire.

Nick I'm going round there. Now.

Martha I would leave it for a while, Nick. She'll be fine.

Hodge If he's not back by midnight I'll come with you. Get a night bus over there.

Nick Will you, Hodge?

Hodge Yeah. It might even be dangerous to disturb them mid-flow. Like sleepwalkers.

Michael Hypnosis interruptus.

Martha What are you drawing, Hodge?

Hodge It's a map of ecstatic moments. Using hieroglyphics and the symbols from the Ordnance Survey.

Michael Did you trace symbols like that on your geisha girl?

Hodge What?

Martha Which geisha girl?

Hodge Nobody.

Michael We went to a Thai massage parlour for Hodge's birthday.

Hodge Michael. Don't. Sorry, Martha.

Martha Tell me about it, Hodge.

Hodge It's months ago. There's nothing to tell. I've forgotten.

Michael Falsification. He remembers it. Every detail. Bamboo chairs. Madame de Fleur.

Martha Who's Madame de Fleur?

Hodge Oh yeah. She was the woman there. She had orchids in her hair.

Martha Really?

Hodge Yeah. The whole place was like a launderette designed by Hokusai.

Martha Seedy?

Hodge No. No it was clean. It smelt of furniture polish. This Madame de Fleur sat us down and gave us all a bottle of beer and took our money. And there were these wooden slatted doors like to a saloon. And they swung open and these five girls walked out. They were all wearing identical short white coats like dental nurses. And they had these calf-length shiny boots on. Different colours. Red. Black. And she said to pick which one we liked and everyone said I should choose first so I pointed to the girl with yellow boots and she took my hand.

Martha Was she the loveliest?

Hodge No. I mean, they were all absolutely stunning. But I thought she probably hadn't chosen those yellow boots. I reckon she was left with them after everyone else had taken theirs. And I went in and she gave me a massage.

Martha And then what?

Hodge Then she asked if I wanted anything else. And I . . . I said yes I would like something else. Yeah. And that was it.

Michael Except you left out the best bit.

Hodge I don't think I did.

Michael So we've all gone into our little rooms and done the business and we come out and have another beer and there's no sign of Hodge. And we wait. And we wait. And Madame de Fleur looks a bit puzzled, and she smiles and goes off to check that everything's okay.

Hodge And it was. It was fine. Everything was fine.

Michael She comes back and tells us that Hodge has been on his knees to this girl from the moment they stepped into that room. He's gone down on her for hours and he's not stopping until she comes. He hasn't fucked her at all.

Hodge starts to tidy up the room.

Martha That's fucking in my book, Michael. Pretty serious fucking.

Michael Yeah, but they just want you in and out there as quick as possible. It's a job. They don't want the secrets of the fucking Perfumed Garden.

Martha How was your girl, Michael?

Michael Yeah, she was great.

Martha Did you imagine she was anyone else while it was happening?

Michael No. Why would I?

Martha You were just saying you had a vivid imagination.

Michael Shall I get some more booze from Tadim's before it shuts?

Hodge There's a whole case downstairs, Michael. Devlin asked me to get one in.

Martha What colour boots did yours wear, Nick?

Nick Hey? Oh. Blue.

Hodge I'm going to make you a blue drink, Martha. A flaming sambuca. Have you ever had one?

Hodge starts to prepare a flaming sambuca for her.

Martha No.

Hodge You're meant to drink it when it's alight from someone's belly button while they lie down on a marble cocktail bar, but I think we might have to stick to mugs.

Hodge gives her the blue flamed drink which he has endeavoured to decorate.

Nick I'm going to have to go round there. What if he tries it on with her?

Michael Fuck's sake, Nick. She's over the age of consent.

Nick She's in a state.

Michael If that meant you couldn't have sex the whole of Britain would be celibate.

Nick Devlin fucked a fifteen-year-old, didn't he? He doesn't have boundaries, does he?

Martha Not especially. Alive is usually enough.

Michael You can't call what he did rape. They were seeing each other. In some countries she'd be married.

Nick Not in this country.

Michael No. Not on this particular blessed isle. And God bless Queen Bess. Why are you getting so fucking sanctimonious?

Nick Adolescents should have sex with people their own age.

Michael And colour? And creed?

Hodge I don't think Nick was advocating eugenics, Michael. He's concerned. About her state of mind.

Nick I'm just expressing my opinion.

Michael Actually you're expressing your own sexual tension.

Nick Fuck you.

Michael What? It was meant very lightly. Tongue-in-cheek.

Nick Maybe I don't want your fucking tongue in my cheek.

Michael You didn't object to it once upon a time, did you?

Nick Fuck off.

Michael Look, why don't you calm down or piss off, Nick? Take your soapbox for a walk.

Nick takes the wine bottle, drinks the remains and walks out.

He's gone. That's better.

Hodge puts a coat over the mannequin and gets his jacket and keys.

Hodge I'd better go and check that he's alright.

Michael Leave him, Hodge. Leave the upright citizen alone.

Hodge No. No, I'd better go.

Hodge exits.

Michael Sorry about Nick. He's a bit uptight.

Martha You act more like his lover than his friend.

Michael Do I? It's not intentional.

Martha How long have you been in love with him?

Michael Sorry? What?

Martha What made you fall for him?

Michael I didn't.

Martha Oh. Okay.

Michael Falling's involuntary, isn't it? It's about encountering a certain geography where your footing goes. Followed by your mind.

Martha And something happened between you?

Michael We spent a night together. Two years ago.

Martha And you're still waiting?

Michael I'm here. This is where I live.

Martha Loitering with intent, then.

Michael Possibly.

Martha Are you hopeful about it?

Michael Yeah. Hope's a terrible thing, Martha.

Martha It is. I always hoped that I'd become my real self when I was with Devlin. It never happened.

Michael I'm myself with Nick. We both are. It doesn't affect our relationship. We work together. Do everything together.

Martha Not everything.

Michael You think I'm mad?

Martha Anyone who's in love is mad. It's wonderful. Do you ever think about leaving?

Michael I do, yeah. Most days. Usually when I'm walking back here. And then I get distracted by how excited I am to be approaching home. Knowing he's here. In one of ten rooms. Or somewhere close by.

Martha You're in a trap.

Michael Yeah. And there's no fear of parting, 'cos we're not together. It's beautiful.

Martha I felt the same about Devlin. He was always bringing back other women. It was like I was living in a fantastic cage.

Michael You think I should move out?

Martha Not necessarily. Love is pretty damn rare. So what if it's not wanted? Doesn't stop you sending it out, does it?

Michael All that unrequited fucking *amore* floating around. It's got to be landing somewhere, hasn't it?

Martha On an exotic uninhabited beautiful island, I should think. Getting caught in palm trees and being examined by spider monkeys.

Michael No wonder they're so fucking animated. Why did you come to see Devlin?

Martha It's necessary. Unfortunately.

Michael You don't want to get back with him?

Martha God, no. I see myself with him in the past now as if it was a terrible silent film. I feel terribly protective over my younger self. Silly, isn't it?

Michael No. Not at all. What did he do that was so wrong?

Martha He wasted my time. And he wasn't kind. I used to lie in the next room and hear him through the walls. Bringing back girls. Always the same routine. Glasses. Cork popping. Lyrical speech pattern. Then the creaking noises. Plosives. Sometimes I even thought I could smell his sweat. What happened the night you and Nick got together?

Michael We'd done a lot of pills. Yeah. I'd given him a couple of 'e's. And it was very . . . memorable.

Martha Did you have sex?

Michael It was . . . intimate. And I don't actually believe you can feel something that intensely unless something's coming back to you as strong from the other person. You'd just feel embarrassed if you were feeling it by yourself, wouldn't you? Exposed. I don't think it can reach that intensity unless it's reciprocated, do you?

Martha No, I don't. Did you talk about it?

Michael No. Never. I hear him fucking the girls he brings back here. I don't actively listen. Well, I did once. (*He puts on music.*) Fuck Devlin. Fuck Nick. Fuck them all. I think we should dance. I think it's the only way. We should have been born as those marathon dancers, you know? If I was a woman, Martha, I'd want to look like you.

Martha If I was a man I'd want to look like you. Let's dance. Let's dance till I have to walk on your feet.

He puts on music and takes Martha up in his arms to dance.

SCENE THREE

Christina's bedsit. Devlin and Christina are drinking coffee, sitting on her bed.

Devlin Was there something wrong with Charlie's leg?

Christina Tracking.

Devlin Is what?

Christina If you inject and it's not pure then it can go toxic. He'd had to buy some stuff on the street because they'd made a mistake with his prescription. When they cut out the septic area it left a hole in his leg. They put in four feet of wadding to fill the gap.

Devlin Shit.

Christina Why did you two lose contact? He was hurt that you'd lost touch with each other.

Devlin My daughter and Charlie were childhood friends. She died. I found it hard to spend time with him afterwards.

Christina Were they close?

Devlin Inseparable. Exquisite muddy savages they were. They got engaged when they were seven by biting into each other's knee until it bled. Teeth marks for weeks on Hildy's left knee. After the accident I felt like I was looking at a dead child every time I went round to take him out. He sensed it.

Christina How old was he?

Devlin Ten. The sharpest age. When your imagination is kicking against being an adult. When people, fuckers, are trying to rip the childhood out of you. He felt that change acutely.

Christina Was he there when Hildy died?

Devlin No. She drowned. In the sea. I was on the beach.
Reading the fantasies of the Marquis de Sade. I was so
concentrated on hiding my erection in the sand that I
didn't notice what was going on. People carried her to
me. And I knew something epic had happened. The sky
had changed colour. Literally. A blue I had never seen
before. She'd be your age now. You mustn't deify Charlie,
you know.

Christina I'm not.

Devlin And his naming me wasn't some code for 'This
was the man who sucked my cock when I was a boy and
that's why I'm ending it all.'

Christina I know that.

Devlin He knew I'd understand. That there should be no
sentiment. No fucking rhetoric or religious chocolate-
box attachment to death. If a child dies, that is a tragedy.
But Charlie wanted to go, and you should celebrate that
with him.

Christina I can't bear that he was alone, Devlin.

Devlin We're all alone. It's just whether we choose to
acknowledge it or not.

Christina I held his hand for a while before you all got
here and it was like damp marble. They'd have lain him
out on a slab afterwards, wouldn't they? No blanket, no
grass. Like a fish they wanted to fillet.

Devlin Absolutely.

Christina Don't you feel any sadness about his death?

Devlin No. I was mercifully anaesthetised on a beach
many years ago and some fucker forgot to take out the
needle. I have no capacity to feel anything.

Christina Nothing?

Devlin Nothing. I'm empty, Christina. Feel.

*He takes her hand and puts it against his heart, then
on to his face and then to his leg. He kisses her hand
and puts her hand to her breast, then touches it
himself. He kisses her. Christina starts to take her
cardigan off. Devlin stops her. He puts her cardigan
back on her.*

Christina I want to.

Devlin No. It's not the right time for you.

Christina You just said I should celebrate.

Devlin Sleep. You should sleep.

Christina Devlin. Please. I have to get rid of this image
in my head. Of Charlie. Please.

*He sits up next to her. The bell buzzes. They do not
respond. It buzzes again. They sit in silence. Christina
turns out the light. The bell buzzes again. And again.
For a prolonged time. A short buzz. Then quiet. A
stone is thrown up at the window.*

Nick (*from outside, shouting*) Christina!

She does not respond.

Devlin!

No response.

Devlin, you fucker!

*Another stone. Then quiet. Then the sustained sound
of the buzzer. Quiet. One last short hopeless buzz.
Then quiet.*

Devlin Is it the Mormons?

Christina No. I thought it might be Charlie.

Devlin It's the other one. He must be fond of you.

Christina Then he's fond of a dead woman. Put your hands around my neck, Devlin.

He does.

Don't let me breathe.

He kisses her.

Stop my mouth. Don't let me breathe.

He kisses her.

SCENE FOUR

The Space. The main lights are out but various lights are on – a flickering fridge light, flashing bike lamps and street lamps. There is loud music. Hodge is sitting transfixed by the music and thought. Michael and Martha are drinking and dancing and are completely out of it. They are throwing themselves into strange dark music full of drums. Nick comes in and is telling Michael that he couldn't get into Christina's. Michael is abandoned and nodding and tries to kiss Nick lightly and passes a joint to him. Nick talks to Martha, who nods and dances. We hear none of their conversation. Nick sits down and stares at them. He gets up and walks out.

SCENE FIVE

Christina's bedsit. Christina is in bed. Devlin is next to her.

Devlin You were talking in your sleep.

Christina About what?

Devlin You said 'I'm scared it will go through to the bone, Charlie.' Then you said 'Thank you for making them smooth.'

Christina He used to shave my legs for me. I was anorexic when we first met and I was always terrified that the razor would sever a vein while I was shaving. So he'd fill that orange bowl with soapy water and he'd sit there and shave them for me. Very gently. By the light of the electric fire. He'd rest his head against my knees. It was the first time someone had really done something for me.

Devlin I should go. Martha will probably be hanging around the studio. Worrying about me.

Christina Yes. Thank you.

Devlin Stop fucking thanking me. I wasn't a magician at your birthday party.

Christina No. Sorry.

Devlin And stop apologising.

Christina Yes. Sorry.

Devlin Errol Flynn used to employ prostitutes. Can you imagine? Errol fucking Flynn? When they asked him why he'd do such a thing, he said he wasn't paying for the sex. He was paying for them to leave in the morning. (*Looking at the objects on the bedside table.*) Are these Charlie's things?

Christina Yes. Every time he came in he'd empty his back pocket. It feels a bit like treasure now. I found his toenail clippings in the bathroom. They suddenly looked Neolithic.

Devlin You couldn't have a lived a life together with him. I asked him once, if he could click something inside him and not need the drugs, would he do it? And he said absolutely not.

Christina I know. You came to one of his lectures, didn't you?

Devlin I did. He was brilliant. Did the image of him go at all? For a moment, anyhow?

Christina Yes. Thank you.

Devlin Liar.

Christina Sorry.

Devlin You look very melancholy. Like a renaissance pietà.

Christina I'm not a pietà, Devlin. I'm a hypocrite.

Devlin We're all hypocrites. If we weren't, there wouldn't be three pairs of friends still talking to each other in the world.

Christina Charlie's illness repulsed me. His compulsive obsession with what his prescription might be that week. Our being together was a lie.

Devlin I'm a liar too.

Christina What do you lie about?

Devlin Anything that pertains to absolutely anything. Will I go? Stay? What should I do?

Christina Whatever you want, Devlin.

Devlin No no. That would be too much.

SCENE SIX

The Space. Hodge is still sitting still. Michael and Martha are dancing to an African mass. They are holding each

*other close and Martha is standing on Michael's feet like
the old marathon dancers. Nick walks in with a bloodied
eye and nose and half a bottle of vodka in his hand. He
sits and watches them. Michael tears off part of his own
shirt. He takes Nick's vodka and pours a little onto the
rag and bathes his cuts. Martha keeps moving to the
music. She takes Nick's hand and leads him up to dance.
They hold each other. Michael joins them and the three
dance together closely. Hodge sits and watches. Now
Martha goes to Hodge and takes him by the hand and
dances close with him. Michael holds Nick tight,
protective, passionate. Hodge is lost in Martha.*

SCENE SEVEN

*Christina's bedsit. Morning. Christina is reading Charlie's
post. The door buzzes.*

Christina Who is it?

Nick Nick.

> *She buzzes him up, opens the door and keeps reading
> the letters. Nick enters with a pint of milk and a
> packet of tea, completely trashed and bruised.*

Nick Morning.

Christina Morning, Nick. God.

Nick How are you?

Christina What happened to your face?

Nick I brought you some tea. Tea.

Christina Thank you.

> *Nick sees the shape of a person in bed.*

Have you had these cuts seen to?

Nick Who's that?

Christina Were you in a fight?

Nick Who is it?

Christina Nobody. Are you going to sit down?

Nick No. He's a cunt. Devlin's a cunt.

Christina Perhaps you should go.

Nick So you two can be on your own? Devlin, you fucker!

Nick goes to the bed and pulls the blankets off to reveal pillows.

Christina Will you have some coffee? Maybe you should go to Casualty. You might need a stitch.

Nick You could do it for me. Sew my cut.

Christina I'm not a nurse.

Nick No. You'd make a beautiful nurse, though. It'd be fantastic waking up next to you and a bowl of fruit, you know? Terrible as well. Torture if you were pulling that curtain round and I wasn't allowed to touch you. Sorry. I'll behave now. I just wanted to say you look great. Really nice. I like the way you do your hair. In a chignon.

Nick sits down. He picks up a prescription.

Did you nurse him a lot?

Christina Sometimes.

Nick How many years was he a junkie?

Christina He was an opiate-dependent.

Nick And was he on something when he died? Or was he clean?

Christina How could he be clean when he was never dirty?

Nick Is that what you think I am? Dirty?

Christina No. I think you're very drunk. And a bit confused.

Nick You're fucking beautiful.

Christina Who hit you?

Nick You did.

Christina Right.

Nick You two didn't fuck any more, did you?

Christina You should go now.

Nick Making that film. Asking me over. It was all to get through to Devlin, wasn't it? So you could reminisce about him together. You're not really going to watch that film. It's not real.

Christina Everything's real, Nick.

Nick No. Some things are real and some things we imagine. We make them up inside our head. That's where we go wrong. Things aren't clear-cut any more. That's real.

He picks up a cup and smashes it against the wall. Nick picks up a fragment and cuts the top of his arm with it.

That's real.

He puts his fingers in the blood and smears it on Christina's face.

That's real. You're so fucking beautiful. Will you put a plaster on my arm? Bathe my cut? Please?

Christina Don't. Don't do that.

Nick It's nothing, Christina. It's nothing. Please don't worry. It's fine. Sorry. We don't feel things. We don't let ourselves feel a thing. There's no sensation. And when I met you that night I felt something. I felt it. I fucking felt it. Fuck it. I still feel it. It's everywhere. In the air. It's like you're in the air. And in my blood.

He takes a bottle of water and he pours half of it over himself.

Christina I'm not. I'm not inside you. I'm not inside anyone. I don't want to be part of anyone. So why don't you just fuck off? How dare you fucking presume that you can decide things about me? Feel things about me when I haven't asked you to? Just fuck off. Leave me alone to do what I want to do.

Christina takes a cup and smashes it. She takes a piece of the debris, but before she can cut herself Nick stops her and takes the shard from her hand and holds her. He kisses her hand and holds her as she tries to push him away. There is almost a fight in how much she wants to get away and how much he wants to hold her. She cries and breaks down fully for the first time. He kneels down in front of her and puts his head to her stomach and holds her.

Nick It's alright. It's all going to be okay.

Christina Is it?

Nick It is.

He leads her to a chair and strokes her back.

Christina I killed him, Nick.

Nick No. No, you didn't.

Christina I wasn't honest with him. And you can't survive if it's a fiction.

Nick Christina. We . . . we slept together the other night. You were asleep and you thought I was Charlie. You'd smoked a lot of dope and you'd taken your sleeping pills and you . . . you thought I was him.

Christina Right.

Nick I'm sorry.

Christina Mm.

Nick Say something. Please.

Christina I watch that drunk Liam from the window. He doesn't stop walking when he crosses the road. The cars all swerve and beep at him and he just nods at them and raises his arms.

Nick I'm sorry, Christina. I'm so sorry.

Christina He reminds me of Jesus walking on water. Because maybe Galilee wasn't calm. Maybe there were broken boats and nets and waves and sewage on the lake. Who's to say that Jesus wasn't a mad pariah fucker like Liam? It's only a question of who's playing the part, isn't it? Robert Powell versus Klaus Kinski.

Nick I'm going now. I'm sorry I smashed your cup. And insulted Charlie. I didn't mean to do that. It all came out wrong. Distorted.

Christina It doesn't matter. No harm done.

Nick No. No. Have you got a dustpan and brush? I love you.

Christina Three days ago you didn't know I existed.

Nick Three days ago some people were alive and now they're dead. Things happen. There's got to be a deciding moment, hasn't there? And my moment about you was instant. Defining. Doesn't make it any less valid.

Christina I'm a bit confused, Nick. I think you probably need to go.

Nick I am. I'm going. But I'm going to come back for you. Please. In six months time. Can I come and see you? Can I do that? Please.

Christina Yes.

Nick I'm sorry I took advantage of you.

Christina You didn't. I was completely aware of both of us the other night, Nick. I didn't think for one moment that you were Charlie.

Nick No?

Christina No. No, I knew it was you I was with. I knew exactly who you were, Nick. I just wished you were him.

He leaves.

SCENE EIGHT

The Space. Dawn. Martha and Hodge are drinking takeaway coffees together. Hodge is drawing on a serviette.

Martha I haven't been up at dawn in a long time.

Hodge I like it. The sounds. And the all-night caffs. Are you tired?

Martha Nicely tired.

Hodge You tell me when you want to go home. I'll get you a cab.

Martha Are you wanting to sleep? Or work?

Hodge No, no. No way I'll sleep. I just meant whatever you want. Are you warm enough?

Martha I am.

Hodge You remind me of Georges Bataille, Martha.

Martha Thanks.

Hodge No. I mean how he talks about ecstasy coming into the world and being part of the atmosphere. That when you die it just comes back into the world. You give a lot. To people.

Martha Some people. You're very beautiful, Tristan.

Hodge I bet you say that to all the girls.

Martha No. I don't. I haven't found someone to be beautiful in a long time.

Hodge Oh. Well. Thanks. Tristan.

Martha What are you drawing?

Hodge I was trying to retrace the steps of how we've come to be sitting here like this. I was thinking if I could graph the map of our ending up on these chairs it would make sense.

Martha Does it have to make sense?

Hodge No. There are these fishes, Martha, who build sandcastles on the sea bed. There's about four hundred male fish to every female. So they compete for her.

Martha They make sandcastles to impress her?

Hodge Yes. They transport the sand in their mouths, so it takes them months to finish it. Then they stand next to their mound and she chooses the winner.

Martha And they swim off together.

Hodge Yeah. But these sculptures they'd made, they had such beautiful details, intricacies. Delicate joins. Can I touch your wrist? Please.

He touches Martha's wrist and forearm.

Your hand is very pure.

Martha Is it?

Hodge Isn't it?

Martha 'Who can find a virtuous woman? For her price is far above rubies.'

Hodge Bible?

Martha Proverbs.

Hodge It's like velvet. Or moss. You remind me of Leonardo's angels.

Martha I don't feel very like an angel.

Hodge I don't expect angels feel very like angels. 'Naturally love is the most distant possibility.' That's what Bataille says.

Martha cries. Hodge puts his arms around her.

Martha? I'm sorry I was quoting some French fucking thinker. I'm not very used to all this.

Martha Sorry. Sorry.

Hodge Don't be sorry. You cry, Martha. Cry as much as you want to. Did I do something wrong?

Martha No, it wasn't you.

Hodge Was it Georges Bataille? Shall I hit him for you?

Martha Tristan.

Hodge Martha.

Martha I don't think I'm who you think I am.

Hodge Well, that's fantastic.

186

Martha I'm a mess.

Hodge You're a beautiful mess. A beatific tangle.

Martha Sometimes I worry.

Hodge Can I do anything to take the worry away?

Martha No. Just hold my hand.

He holds her hand.

Hodge Martha.

Martha Yes.

Hodge I've never had such a night. Before.

Martha It was a wonderful night Tristan.

Hodge Will we . . .?

Martha Will we?

Hodge Can I take you somewhere today? After you've slept. Anywhere.

Martha I need to be home. By half past three.

Hodge Before that, then. Can I take you out? Where's your favourite place?

Martha I like the river. And I like visiting the Virgin and St Anne at the National Gallery. I like to sit and watch them until they start to move.

Hodge Yeah? I used to do that, too.

Martha You can get very lost in her face.

Hodge You can. Are you hungry?

Martha I am.

Hodge I'll make up my bed for you and get some bagels from Brick Lane. Do you like bagels?

Martha I love bagels.

Hodge Oh. I'm feeling quite jealous now. Of inanimate bread objects.

Martha Can I have some coffee too?

Hodge You can. You can have anything you want.

Martha I want you.

Hodge What?

Martha You heard.

Hodge Would you say it once more? Please. For posterity.

Martha I. Want. You.

Hodge smiles, nods, kisses her wrist and leaves.

SCENE NINE

Christina's bedsit. Christina has been crying. She is pasting cuttings into a book. She sings.

Christina
'What can I give him,
Poor as I am?
If I were a shepherd
I would give a lamb.
If I were a wise man,
I would do my part,
Yet what I can I give him?
Give my heart.'

SCENE TEN

The Space. Michael and Hodge are washing the floors.

Hodge It's a waste of time.

Michael What?

Hodge The dirt's ingrained now. We need to strip it and paint it, then varnish it.

Michael We don't need to eat off it, Hodge. I got an email from East. Which paintings should we show them, do you think?

Hodge East? Yes. I just had a coffee with Martha.

Michael I don't know whether we should take along the large-scale stuff or if that would scare them off.

Hodge Where's Nick?

Michael No idea.

Hodge We haven't repainted it since we've been here.

Michael Strictly speaking you've never been here, Hodge. It's not your space. It was always mine and Nick's. You're very welcome here, you know that, but that's the way it is.

Hodge I've never wanted to be more than a collaborator. And we were discussing the floor, not who's running the place.

Michael Yeah. Exactly.

Hodge He doesn't want you.

Michael What?

Hodge Nick.

Michael What the fuck are you on about, Hodge?

Hodge It's just that I know the language of rejection. Intimately. And one fact can sometimes be more helpful than a hundred signs or clues.

Michael Thanks for the advice. I don't know what the hell you're on about. And of course you're known as Casa-fucking-nova around here, aren't you? On account of your sexual prowess.

Hodge Who called me that? Someone today?

Michael No. Nobody ever called you it.

Hodge I'm not a virgin.

Michael I'm not Elvis Presley.

Hodge No, I mean since last night. With Martha.

Michael What? Seriously?

Hodge Yeah.

Michael Fuck. Hodge. Hodge. Really? How was it?

Hodge Oh yeah, well, it was, you know . . . fantastic, yeah. Exquisite. Three times. Yeah.

Michael Christ. Shit. That's brilliant. Shit. Three times.

Hodge Yeah, yeah actually. A holy trinity. Not that I was counting.

Michael That's just fantastic.

Hodge Thanks, Mike. Yeah, she's liberated me from a lifetime of eternal carrier bags and comics.

Michael Martha's fucking gorgeous.

Hodge Yeah, well, you know.

Michael It's great. That's amazing. I'm really sorry,

Hodge. I'm sorry I was a twat.

Hodge No no, that's fine.

Michael What I said about the Space. You know it's yours too. I was just being fucking mardy.

Hodge I didn't really listen to what you were saying, actually. I was just thinking about Martha.

Devlin walks in.

Devlin Who was thinking about Marta?

Hodge Nobody.

Devlin So what is this? Some sort of kabuki ritual?

Michael No. We always do it before openings.

Hodge I've got part of your fee here, Devlin.

He gives him an envelope with some notes in it and a transparent carrier bag full of small change.

They've got a machine at Sainsburys if you want to change that up. I'm getting some teas in. Do you want anything? A doughnut?

Devlin No. It will remind me that there is something missing. I took a couple of bagels from the tower someone has constructed in the kitchen. Must be a hundred of them there. It wasn't an installation, was it? I haven't eaten the art?

Michael Yeah. What the hell is that?

Hodge A tower? Oh yeah, well, maybe the mice built it.

Devlin You're very ebullient today.

Hodge Yes. I'm very hungry. I could eat a shire horse.

Martha enters.

Good morning, Martha.

Martha Hello, Hodge. What's that in the kitchen?

Hodge Do you like it?

Martha Very much. What's it called?

Hodge 'The Tower of Bagel'.

Martha And what does it represent?

Hodge It's a meditation on the notion of ecstasy. Its alternative title is 'Four Hundred Fish and She Chose Me.'

Hodge leaves and Michael follows him.

Devlin I'm sorry if I was cruel the other night, Marta. I don't remember what I said. But I suspect it was the same-old same-old. Repetitious I know. Should be like water off a swan's back to you.

Martha It was fine.

Devlin You came to find me and I wasn't here? I'm sorry if you had a sleepless night.

Martha I enjoy a sleepless night now and again..

Devlin Thank you. Benevolent as ever. I can't go through with this bloody weekend. Can you tell them for me, Marta? I'll keep the fee. I don't want them thinking well of me. I've gone to trouble anyway so technically it's mine.

Martha Where will you go?

Devlin Home. Back to exile in Bermondsey, courtesy of the Peabody Trust. I'll see you, Marta.

He kisses her forehead and starts to leave.

Martha We had a child, Devlin.

Devlin What?

Martha We have a child. I've been wanting to tell you.

Devlin What?

Martha We spent that night together in Dublin.

Devlin Yes.

Martha And I had a child.

Devlin No. You what? You had a child?

Martha I didn't tell you at the time because you'd been such an absolute bastard. Then I heard about Hildy, so I decided to tell you later.

Devlin Twelve years later.

Martha I tried to tell you. That's why I came to see you in prison. But you weren't yourself in there. You were so disorientated when I visited. I thought I'd wait until you came out. And I wrote you all those letters which you didn't reply to and I started to wonder if you needed to know about Tom.

Devlin Tom?

Martha Yeah. He's a fantastic boy. He wants to be an explorer.

Devlin We have a child.

Martha We do.

Devlin And he's called Tom.

Martha Yes. After my brother.

Devlin And he wants to be an explorer. You didn't tell me.

Martha No. We went to Sofia to find you but no one knew which part of the countryside you'd moved to. I've always talked to him about you. I told him the other day that I'd heard you were back in London. And he said he wanted to meet you.

Devlin Yes.

Martha Would you? Like to meet him?

Devlin Marta.

Martha You should, Devlin. He's a funny thing. Very intense. He loves Airfix models. His hands shake when he makes them, he's such a perfectionist.

Devlin Fucking hell, Marta.

Martha Yes, I know. Will you come round and see him? He's brilliant.

Devlin Good. That's very good. But I don't think so.

Martha You don't think so? He's not an idea, Devlin. He's a boy.

Devlin I had a child. I have no need of another. And this is hardly a fair position to put me in, Marta.

Martha You haven't any imagination, have you?

Devlin What? You're probably right. You were always right.

Martha I don't want to be right. I just want you to meet him. I couldn't care less if I never saw you again. But he wants to see you and he has that right. And meeting him could only be joyful. He's a very joyful boy.

Devlin Perhaps we could all meet the once. I could walk him round the National Gallery and explain the paintings?

Martha No. Just tea. And chips or something. At mine. Something simple.

Devlin Simple. Yes. A child.

Martha Tom. He looks at people the same way you do. The questions he asks are similar, too.

Devlin Does he drink?

Martha Not yet. He's a brilliant draughtsman.

Devlin Have you asked him to draw Giotto's perfect circle?

Martha It must have slipped my mind.

Devlin Tommy?

Martha No. Tom.

SCENE ELEVEN

Nick and Michael are in the Space, shredding papers.

Michael He's not a painter. He's a schmuck. He redefines the notion of awkward. And demanding. He wastes our time for three months. Twelve weeks we've been writing about this. Now he asks me to shred all our communications. As if anyone gives a shit what he said in his lunatic emails, anyhow. What the hell does it look like inside his head? Do you think taking up our time gives him a sense of importance?

Nick Maybe.

Michael You're not really bothered, are you?

Nick I liked meeting him.

Michael We could have met the man over a pint down the road.

Nick Do you still love painting, Michael?

Michael Course I do, yeah.

Nick Just we never seem to paint now. It's become about where it'll end up rather than what it is.

Michael We provide a brilliant space for people. Free. That's important.

Nick I said I'd stay away from her for six months.

Michael It's probably a good idea. If you can manage it.

Nick Yeah. I told her to call me if she needed to. But she hasn't.

Michael It's only been a day, Nick.

Nick Yeah. Felt like quite a long day, though. I actually think I'm going a bit mad.

Michael Go and see her. Tell her how you feel.

Nick Yeah?

Michael Get a train to Streatham. Sit down and have a quick drink in a local Firkin or Frigate or whatever. Then go and talk to her.

Nick Is that what you'd do?

Michael Yeah.

Nick Really?

Michael Yeah. Except I wouldn't need to go to Streatham to say it.

SCENE TWELVE

Christina's bedsit. Christina is knitting. A knock on the door.

Christina It's open.

Nick walks in.

Nick Hi.

Christina Hi.

Nick What you knitting?

Christina A scarf.

Nick Great. How are you?

Christina I'm a day older. You?

Nick Okay. Who's the scarf for?

Christina Devlin. He asked me to make him something.

Nick Oh.

Christina How was your day?

Nick Good. Yeah, fantastic.

Christina Painting?

Nick Shredding. Who's the scarf for?

Christina You just asked me that.

Nick Yeah. I didn't mean to ask you that. It was meant to come out as something else.

Christina Yes. Do you want some tea?

Nick No. No tea. What you been doing?

Christina Knitting. Looking out the window. I was watching the trees out there go crazy with the wind.

Nick Yeah, it's mad weather, isn't it?

Christina I've been watching people. Walking down the road. It's been cold, hasn't it?

Nick Freezing. The space is like an igloo.

Christina Do you cut holes in the middle of the floor and look for fish?

Nick Yeah. And we've got a couple of seals in the corner too.

Christina Good.

Nick Christina. I need to know if . . . No no, I don't need to know anything.

Christina If what?

Nick Nothing. I'm not asking you for anything. Not now. Not for ages. I just wondered if I should wait for you? If you'd like me to wait.

Christina Does it have to be a definite yes or no?

Nick Yes. Unless it's a no, in which case it can be a variation.

Christina Nick . . .

Nick Christina.

Christina I do find it very hard to accept love. I do. Find it hard.

Nick That's okay. The important things aren't easy, are they? I mean, I support Southampton. That's not always easy.

Christina Isn't it?

Nick No. It's fucking heartbreaking. So is there hope?

Christina There's always hope.

Nick No. No, there isn't.

Christina In this case there's hope.

Nick Devlin was reading us some of Rumi's poems. One

of them said that God made Majnun love Layla so much that even her dog caused confusion in him.

Christina That's nice.

Nick Yeah. Even her dog.

SCENE THIRTEEN

The Space. Michael is at his computer. He listens to a tape on his Dictaphone and repeats the Arabic phrases.

Tape Leave me alone. *Utruknee waHdee.*

Michael *Utruknee waHdee.*

Tape I'm ill. *Ana mareeD.*

Michael *Ana mareeD.*

Tape I'm lost. *Ana tuht.*

Michael *Ana tuht.*

Tape Where are the bathrooms? *Ayn al-Hammaamaat.*

Michael *Ayn al- Hammaamaat.*

SCENE FOURTEEN

Martha and Devlin are in a street.

Devlin What's he run off for?

Martha He wanted to buy you a present. With his pocket money.

Devlin Tell him next time I'd just prefer the pocket money.

Martha How was it for you?

Devlin Did you tell him to do that? To call me Dad?

Martha Course I didn't.

Devlin Chasing me round the Brueghel rooms shouting 'Dad ! What's that, Dad?' It was surreal, Marta.

Martha It's lovely that he can be so open. People must have thought you were the paragon of a parent.

Devlin He'd never heard of Giotto. What have you been teaching him?

Martha A lot of useless information. Do you like him, Devlin?

Devlin What kind of a stupid question is that?

Martha Do you?

Devlin He's everything, isn't he? Beauty. Innocence. Spirit. How could one not like him?

Martha So you'll see him again?

Devlin If he wants to see me. But it's his choice, of course.

Martha I think he will want to see you.

Devlin Do you? Do you think so?

Martha Yes. I do. He was talking about it.

Devlin Right. Good. I'm not taking him to see those fucking sharks at the aquarium, though. Huge white death's heads.

Martha They are in tanks, Devlin.

Devlin Everything's fallible, Marta. He's inherited your looks. Poor fella might have my nose, though.

Martha Your nose is very fine.

Devlin Is it? It's not bad, is it? It's better seen from the left, actually. I told him I couldn't paint any more. He was so intelligent about it. Incisive.

Martha What did he say?

Devlin He just nodded. We sat there saying nothing for a bit. Then he put his arm around me for a moment. Like a monkey. With his red backpack.

He takes Martha's hand.

Martha Do you think we'll ever stop, Devlin?

Devlin Stop what?

Martha Stop trying. Do you think we'll ever stop trying and just be ourselves?

Devlin Surely the act of trying is being ourselves.

Martha No. I don't think it is. But trying's rather beautiful in itself, isn't it?

Devlin It is. Marta. It is.

Martha Martha.

Devlin Martha.

Martha Martha.

Lights down.

HER NAKED SKIN

For my mother, Celia
(Mouse)

'I freeze and yet am burned'
Elizabeth I

Her Naked Skin was first performed in the Olivier auditorium of the National Theatre, London, on 24 July 2008. The cast was as follows:

Celia Cain Lesley Manville
William Cain Adrian Rawlins
Eve Douglas Jemima Rooper
Florence Boorman Susan Engel
Mrs Schliefke Pamela Merrick
Emily Wilding Davison Zoë Aldrich

HOUSE OF COMMONS
Herbert Asquith David Beames
Miss Brint Harriette Quarrie
John Seely Julien Ball
Augustine Birrell Ken Bones
Edward Grey Simon Markey
Keir Hardie Robert Willox

HOLLOWAY PRISON
Potter Tony Turner
Mrs Briggs Stephanie Jacob
Dr Vale Dermot Kerrigan
Dr Parker Nick Malinowski
Nurse Elicia Daly
Young Nurse Stephanie Thomas
Wardress Ruth Keeling
Guard Edward Newborn
Guard Joe Dunlop

Charlie Power Gerard Monaco
Hunt Julien Ball
Brown Tony Turner
Doctor Klein Ken Bones
Mrs Collins Deborah Winckles
Lord Curzon David Beames
Robert Cecil Robert Willox
Mrs Major Barbara Kirby
Felicity Anna Lowe

Other parts played by members of the Company

Director Howard Davies
Designer Rob Howell
Lighting Designer Neil Austin
Projection Designer Jon Driscoll
Music Harvey Brough
Sound Designer Paul Groothuis
Assistant Director Elly Green

Characters

Celia Cain
forties

Florence Boorman
seventies

Eve Douglas
twenties

Mrs Schliefke
sixties

Mrs Briggs
twenties

Miss Brint
twenties

Mrs Collins
sixties

Emily Wilding Davison
forties

Mary Nicholson
twenties

Clara Franks
twenties

William Cain
forties

Charlie Power
twenties

Brown
forties

Hunt
forties

Keir Hardie
fifties

Herbert Asquith
sixties

John Seely
fifties

Edward Grey
fifties

Augustine Birrell
fifties

George Curzon
fifties

Robert Cecil
fifties

Dr Klein
forties

Dr Vale
thirties

Dr Parker
twenties

Potter
thirties

**Guards, Nurse, Suffragettes,
Wardresses and MPs**
Parts may be doubled/tripled

The action takes place in London in 1913

Act One

SCENE ONE

A parlour. Morning. Emily Wilding Davison sits, dressed to go outside. She stands and puts a sash around her waist in front of a mirror. She turns on the gramophone. A contemporary song plays. She checks herself in the mirror and touches the lining of her jacket. The gramophone gets stuck. She does not move. She checks the lining of her jacket again. She takes the needle off the record, checks her purse, goes to the mirror, puts on her hat and checks the inside of her jacket. She picks up a rolled piece of paper then leaves with it in her hand.

The sound of a gramophone needle on a cracked old record going round, loud.

On a large screen we see the Derby of 1913. The horses race around Tattenham Corner and a small grainy figure comes onto the track and is trampled underfoot. The image is almost impossible to make out but the general impression of the film is that something has 'happened'.

SCENE TWO

The House of Commons. A private room. Afternoon. Some of Asquith's cabinet sit at a large table, smoking, drinking. It is an informal summoning of Liberal MPs. Birrell and Grey pass round photographs and newspapers. Seely enters and takes a seat.

Seely Temperature's gone sky high, no?

Birrell Thought we had a cold, turns out to be a fever.

Seely At least they've laid on a drink.

Grey Has anyone actually talked to him yet?

Seely I just passed him on the stairway. He looked like it was war to the knife.

Grey Curzon's gone loco about it too. Says we should deport them.

Seely Yes. Well. Curzon.

Asquith enters. He is with a young female secretary, Miss Brint.

Grey Sir.

Asquith Grey.

Asquith sits. Miss Brint sits apart from the MPs.

So? What are we thinking?

Seely It'll burn itself out, H.H. A few days of women keening, then it'll die down.

Asquith I think you're being optimistic.

Birrell I'm with you. I don't think it's going away. It's all dependent, of course.

Asquith Yes. Quite.

Birrell Hardie will jump on it tomorrow.

Grey If it becomes heated in the House, Seely simply comes in with the Irish.

Seely There's enough to come in with.

Grey examines the picture.

Grey Pluck.

Asquith What?

Grey Got to give it to her. The girl has pluck.

Asquith I don't believe her pluck is in dispute. Any word, Miss Brint?

Brint Miss Davison's unlikely to survive the day, sir.

Asquith That's . . . unfortunate.

Grey Damn miracle the gal's lasted this long.

Asquith Bugger. There'll be a major funeral, no?

Birrell It'll be women as far as the eye can see.

Asquith Which should sound like heaven, but it doesn't.

Quiet smiles and chuckles at the PM's wit.

Grey Our man at Poplar says they're planning a march, thousands of them.

Asquith A touch tasteless. And premature. What does the *Post* say?

Birrell examines its front page.

Birrell Queen enquired about Miss Davison's progress last night. They're calling the latest attacks an 'epidemic'.

Grey They scorched my golf course, did I tell you? Acid all over the grass. Rare finches there, too. I don't expect they relished the amazon invasion.

Birrell (*reads*) 'Militant suffragism is like a pain in the body . . . monomania.'

Asquith You say she's tried it before?

Asquith looks to Miss Brint who looks to her notes.

Brint Yes, sir. From the prison balcony. Twice.

Grey Hysterical.

Asquith That's what we'll have to concentrate on. Her lack of . . .

Birrell A horse? Sorry, just came out.

Seely If we brand her a hysteric we may suffer a backlash.

Birrell The real problem is, the public will renew their focus on the forcible feeding.

Asquith Hospital treatment, Birrell.

Birrell Call it what you like. There'll be a new stink all over again. If this woman dies they've got their first bona fide martyr. It may well blow their non-violent manifesto to kingdom come.

Seely I think you're being a touch dramatic.

Birrell They keep comparing their campaign to the Irish. Look where that's headed.

Asquith The Irish are the Irish. And they've been damned useful to us. What we're dealing with here is a lunatic fringe of lonely frigid women who crave attention. Anything new from the police?

Brint They found a return ticket in her purse, sir. And a diary entry for next week.

Pause. Hard thought while Asquith refills his glass.

Seely That's rather good, isn't it? Ergo, she didn't mean to die for the cause at all. She stepped out onto the track by mistake.

Brint What?

Seely What?

Brint Nothing. Sorry, sir.

Grey My mother had no sense of direction whatsoever. Still stretching it a bit though, isn't it?

A few stolen looks behind Brint's back. Veiled chuckles.

Seely People run out onto the course after all the horses have gone by.

Birrell You're saying she might not have seen forty thoroughbreds racing round Tattenham Corner at full pelt?

Seely I'm saying she was endeavouring to celebrate in the traditional fashion. But was a little premature. What do you think?

Asquith pours himself a stronger drink.

Asquith Maybe she'll live. That would be better, wouldn't it? (*Pause.*) Wouldn't it?

Seely Absolutely. Of course. It would be wonderful. Preservation of human life aside, which we all pray will happen, it would . . .

Grey Indicate a botch job. Universal female incompetence. Present company excepted. Right up to the tenth hole they scorched it. Rotten.

Asquith You're right, Seely. People will see it as nothing compared to Ireland. So who's making the big noise about Home Rule tomorrow?

SCENE THREE

Regent Street. Evening. Celia Cain stands near a shop front. There are various women, looking in windows, along the street. A Flower Lady stands next to a Newspaper Vendor. Eve Douglas watches Celia.

Celia Do you have the time upon you, please?

The Vendor gets out his watch.

Vendor Just coming up to six.

Celia How many minutes to six?

Vendor How many? . . . Seven.

Celia Thank you. I'll have a paper, please.

Celia gives the Vendor a coin and takes the paper. Eve approaches Celia.

Eve Excuse me. Are you? . . . Sorry. Nothing.

Celia Yes. I expect I am.

Eve Oh.

Celia Yes.

Celia walks away from Eve and approaches the Flower Seller.

I'll have some violets, please.

Flower Seller Ta.

The Flower Seller wraps some violets for Celia, who takes them and walks away. Eve approaches Celia again.

Eve I'm . . . I . . .

Celia What? Is it your first time? I promise it won't hurt.

Eve I don't think I can do it.

Celia Excuse me.

Celia walks away from Eve and stands near another shop. Celia looks at the newspaper, distracted. She puts the newspaper under her arm, waits. Eve watches

214

*her, then takes out a hammer and smashes the
window in front of her.*

Eve I did it. I did it.

Celia Yes. You're a touch bloody early, but you did it.

*Celia takes out a hammer from her coat and smashes
the shop window in front of her. The other women in
the street follow suit. Windows are being smashed
simultaneously throughout the West End.*

SCENE FOUR

*Florence, Mrs Schliefke and other Suffragettes line up in
front of a prison guard, Potter, who sits at a table and
writes down their details. Once they have answered
Potter's questions they go to a set of scales and are
weighed. A Guard records their weight. Then on to
another table where a Guard issues them with items such
as a toothbrush and a handkerchief.*

Potter Name?

Mary Nicholson Mary Nicholson.

Potter Occupation.

Mary Nicholson Factory worker.

Potter Sentence.

Mary Nicholson Seven months. Windows.

Potter Name.

Clara Franks Clara Franks.

Potter Occupation.

Clara Franks Student of fine art.

Potter Sentence.

Clara Franks Six months.

Potter Name.

Florence Florence Dorothy Mary Boorman.

Potter Occupation.

Florence Suffragist.

Potter Occupation, Miss Boorman. Not offence.

Florence Suffragist. Suffragette. Womanist. Woman. That's what I'm occupied with at the present moment in time and have been for the past sixty years.

Potter Employment.

Florence Suffragette. Sentence seven months.

Potter Can't get enough of it, can you?

Florence I was on marches before you were born.

Potter Which just goes to show how long and ineffectual your campaign has been.

Florence Which division are you putting us in?

Potter Second.

Florence We are politicals. Not thieves or child-killers. We should be placed in first.

Potter (*indicating his form*) Criminal damage. See.

Florence The tide is changing, Potter. Watch out. The water will come rushing in under your feet and you'll find you won't have a pot to piss in. If you insist on placing us in second, you'd better arrange for the prison glazier now. We will immediately proceed to break our windows. It is our legal right to be in first. Visitors we should have, pens, paper. Associated labour. Permitted access to other cells.

Celia and Eve Douglas enter and join the line.

Potter Nobody's listening. Why don't you give it a rest, Miss Boorman?

Florence Why don't you get yourself a proper job? Instead of collecting birds and putting them in cages. It's more the act of a deranged child than an evolved man, I must warn you. But still I wish you luck.

Potter With what?

Florence You don't have the vote, Potter? No wonder your aspirations are so low. I wish you all the best in the fight for universal suffrage. Any news on Miss Davison?

Potter Name.

Eve Eve Douglas.

Potter Occupation.

Eve Machinist tailor. In Limehouse.

Potter Sentence.

Eve Seven months. Windows.

Potter Name.

Celia You know my name. I know your name.

Potter Name.

Celia Lady Celia Madeline Ottoline Cain.

Potter Occupation.

Celia looks at him, he writes something down. Celia carries some undergarments.

Sentence.

Celia Is there a wardress about, Potter?

No reply.

No matter, you're practically family. An honorary woman by now.

Potter Are you taking me off?

Celia I'm quite serious. I've never been issued undergarments like these before. They've stains in places I don't wish to contemplate. Any chance of some replacement duds? And there wasn't a pair of shoes to be had in the basket so the left one is killing me. I feel like a bloody geisha. Potter? I'm not invisible.

Potter What exactly is it that you want?

Celia What I want is a crêpe-de-chine nightgown and glass slippers. What I'm asking for are undergarments that don't look and smell like someone died in them. Plus two shoes of a similar size. And we would very much like to know how our comrade Emily Wilding Davison is doing. Do you read the papers? She's been unconscious for three days after throwing herself in front of the King's horse. I thought you might have seen the article, even if you only go straight to the sports section.

Potter ignores the request. Celia joins the other women who are assembled in a line waiting for their cell allocation. Potter looks to the Guard.

Potter Get the next lot in.

Celia joins the other women, who are assembled in a line waiting for their cell allocation. Potter continues to write.

Florence How are you feeling now, Mrs Schliefke?

Mrs Schliefke What? I don't suppose we'll have an eyelash left when they're through with us.

Celia It's just about getting used to the frowsy clothes now. Last time we were here Florence tried to steal her hospital slippers when we got out. They weren't even a pair, were they?

Florence I'd formed a bizarre attachment to them. (*To Potter.*) Which just goes to show how quickly one can become institutionalised! Have you visited the zoological gardens, Potter? Do you see what happens to those beasts? They pace up and down. They eat their own tails and faeces. They lose their fur. They make noises in their cages that should only be heard in hell. Their only crime was being rare or beautiful. As is ours, sir. As is ours.

Potter I grant you you're rare, Boorman.

Florence picks up her toothbrush and joins the other women.

Mrs Schliefke One hears it's very healthy to express one's self. It actually prolongs life. I'm rather worried. That I've offended God.

Celia You don't think He's a feminist? I suspect you're right.

Mrs Schliefke It wasn't a very Christian act, was it?

Florence We're smashing up glass, not people.

Mrs Schliefke But still. I can't reconcile it. Turn the other cheek, he said.

Florence You can't very well turn your cheek when you're being held face down in the mud.

Mrs Schliefke I just find it sad. That it's created such a division in the ranks. That discussion couldn't prevail.

Florence You can't discuss something if you're refused a voice, can you?

Mrs Schliefke No. No. Ignore me. I'm too tired to move. No swagger.

Eve Can you get tobacco in here?

Celia You can procure pretty much anything if you've the cash. You did it, then?

Eve What happens in second division?

Florence You're on your own for twenty-three hours of the day. Did you bring a pencil?

Eve No.

Florence breaks the cotton of her petticoat hem, produces a pencil and gives it to Eve without Potter seeing.

Florence Write on the walls. Demand associated labour. And smash your windows if they don't open.

Potter That's enough! You be quiet else you'll go straight to isolation! Now!

Florence I'll be quiet when I die.

Potter Which is what your friend is. Dead.

Florence Dead? When?

Potter Today.

Florence Today. Oh.

A Guard enters.

Mary Nicholson Her skull was smashed in.

Clara Franks It was.

Mrs Schliefke May we go to the chapel, sir, and say a prayer for our sister?

Guard They're ready for them now. Block DX.

Potter You can pray in your cells. Go on then. Piss off.

A Guard leads them away.

SCENE FIVE

Holloway Prison. Night. In various cells in the shadows, women take down their plank beds from the wall and make them up with a blanket. A gas lamp burns in each cell. Briggs does the rounds. She rattles the door of each cell with her keys and shouts; each prisoner must come to the door and reply to her enquiry. Another Wardress sits on their corridor, knitting.

Briggs Alright?

Mrs Schliefke Alright.

At the next cell.

Briggs Alright?

Eve I haven't got a blanket. And can I have the light out, please? I can't turn it down from in here.

At the next cell.

Briggs Alright?

Celia I'm minus a blanket too.

The Wardress unlocks Celia's gate. Then unlocks Eve's.

Briggs Wait. Wait.

The Wardress continues her routine.

Alright?

Florence Alright.

Briggs exits to fetch blankets.

Celia (*to Eve*) They never put the light out.

Eve How long you in for?

Celia Three months. You?

Eve Seven.

Celia What do you do?

Eve I'm a machinist. I do collars.

Celia Is it sweated?

Eve They all are. I'd murder for a smoke.

Celia Who would you kill?

Briggs enters with the blankets.

Briggs Shut up, Douglas! Cain. Blanket.

Celia Did anyone ever tell you that you have a wonderful facility for language, Briggs?

Briggs In. Now.

Celia I'm just curious. Do you think you're actually saving time by leaving words out?

Briggs holds the door open for Celia, who walks in. Briggs shuts and locks it, checks that Eve is in her cell, then shuts and locks it.

SCENE SIX

The Prison. Night time. A doctor's office is lit brightly. Dr Vale and Dr Parker set up their equipment. A Nurse lays a white sheet under an armchair. She rearranges it so that it is flat and neat. Dr Vale pours liquid into a jug from a larger one. Dr Parker cleans a long red rubber tube. Dr Vale whistles 'The Man Who Broke the Bank at Monte Carlo'.

Vale Unbearable heat, isn't it?

Parker Stifling.

Vale You've not done this business before, no?

Parker I haven't. Is there anything I should know?

Vale Basic procedure. It's somewhat tougher here than at the asylum. They can be a bit bullish.

The Nurse has finished laying the sheet down.

Nurse Is there anything else you need, Dr Vale?

Vale No, Nurse. You shuffle off home if they let you out.

Nurse Yes, Doctor. Goodbye.

Parker Goodbye, Nurse.

The Nurse exits.

Vale I'm going to the Criterion tonight. Is it any good, do you know?

Parker Underhill said there can be complications. Pneumonia?

Vale Occasionally. Pleurisy's the killer of course. If the liquid goes down the wrong way. Ends up in the lungs. Fatal when it happens. One does entreat them to recant. Up to the eleventh hour they can walk out of here untouched. Stubborn, you see. They're very stubborn. Tomorrow. Don't wear your best suit. Can you put out the light?

Parker turns the gas down and the Doctors exit.

SCENE SEVEN

The Prison kitchen. Morning. Various Suffragettes are on work duty. Celia and Eve peel a vast pile of potatoes together. Once peeled they put them in a huge pot filled with water. Briggs loiters and walks around inspecting the workers.

Eve You don't smoke, do you?

Celia No.

Eve I keep thinking about Miss Davison. Did you know her?

Celia No.

Eve Do you smoke?

Celia No. You just asked me that.

Eve Sorry.

Celia I tried it once. Couldn't get the measure of it.

Eve There's nothing to it. I'll show you one day. Gorgeous, it is. Are you going on strike?

Celia Tomorrow.

Eve You done it before?

Celia Quite a bit. But I've never been pulled in for the feeding.

Eve They sound more like they're being slaughtered than fed.

Celia Yes, it's not very clever.

Eve I keep wondering if she was lonely. When she went out there. Walking out in front of all those crowds.

Holding her arm up like that with those great big horses
going past her. I hope she didn't regret it at the last
moment. It's funny to be part of something. I've never
been part of anything before.

Celia It's rather wonderful, isn't it?

Eve Yeah. Besides the actual prison side of it.

Celia Besides the stench. And the noise at night. And the
dog soap.

Eve finds dog soap funny.

Eve Dog soap.

Celia Besides that it's rather wonderful.

*They laugh. Eve puts a potato in and drops her knife
with it. She starts to feel for it.*

Lost your knife?

Eve Yeah.

*They feel slowly and carefully for the knife; their
hands bump into each other's in the vat and they
continue to search in the muddied water until Celia
produces it.*

Celia There.

Eve Ta. I'm a bit scared I'll lose my bottle. If they get me
in for the feeding.

Celia There's no shame if you do. Don't be too harsh
upon yourself. You're terribly young.

Eve Not really. Beautiful, aren't they? Children.

Celia They are. Do you have any?

Eve No. Not married. You?

Celia Actually I'd prefer not to talk about such things.

Eve Oh.

Celia I'm married to God. I was part of the Poor Clare convent before all of this.

Eve Oh.

Celia I'm a virgin.

Celia smiles at Eve. Celia laughs.

Eve You're not a nun. What's your name?

Briggs Talking! No talking!

Celia Celia. May I call you by your first name?

Eve Eve. As in the garden.

They smile. Silence. They keep peeling the potatoes.

SCENE EIGHT

*The House of Commons. Afternoon. Question Time.
Keir Hardie addresses the Prime Minister, Herbert
Asquith. The Speaker presides. Members of Parliament
make the usual white noise.*

Speaker Pray silence for the Honourable Member for
Merthyr Tydfil, Keir Hardie.

Hardie Prime Minister, when will you put a stop to the
forcible feeding of the militant section of the women's
suffrage movement in Holloway Prison?

*The usual Question Time cacophony that sounds
vaguely like a farmyard and has a flavour of derision
to it.*

Asquith We are simply keeping these women alive.
Should this hospital treatment stop they would starve
and we have no desire for any more suffragette martyrs.

Hardie Might I remind the Honourable Gentlemen of the House that the last death connected to a hunger strike was in 1870. And the prisoner in question died not from the fasting but as a result of the forcible feeding. These women are political prisoners. What they are being subjected to is an illegal process. They are worn and weak with hunger. In this condition they are seized upon and held down by anything up to ten persons. Are you aware, sir, that a steel gag is often enforced? It is lodged between their teeth to keep their mouth open?

An MP I would have thought the primary objective would be to keep those women's mouths shut!

A loud guffaw from the others.

Speaker Order! Order!

Hardie I have enquired before under what law this feeding was done, but Mr Masterman was unable to say without notice. Only that it was by order of the Home Office. My understanding was that this enforcement was for those certified to be insane.

An MP Quite right! Bloody madwomen!

More guffaws.

Hardie If women die from this the blood is on your hands, Prime Minister. Might I say the behaviour of the House today and on days previous to this when I have asked this question has been deeply shocking and repugnant. Had I not heard the laughter myself I could not have believed that a body of gentlemen could have found reason for mirth and applause in a scene which I venture to say has no parallel in the recent history of our country.

An MP Go home to your washing!

An MP Home to your washing! Home to your washing!

Guffaws.

Speaker Order! Order!

Hardie I put it to you, sir, their lives are in your hands. Shame on our society for letting this happen. Let British men think over this spectacle.

Asquith I can only repeat that these women are in Holloway of their own volition. And their refusal to eat is at their own behest.

'Hear, hear!'s from the benches.

Speaker I believe there was a pressing question about taxation from the bench?

SCENE NINE

Holloway Prison. Evening. Women lie on their beds or sit on the floors in their cells.
  Celia sits in her cell, reading; she wears glasses. Briggs unlocks the door and enters.

Briggs I didn't know you wore spectacles, Lady Cain.

Celia Yes. I try to use them sparingly. I think they're rather unbecoming.

Briggs Literary. Very nice.

Celia Thank you, Briggs. Was there . . . something?

Briggs Your husband, miss.

Celia Yes? What about him?

Briggs He's here, miss. To see you.

Celia Here? My husband?

Briggs Yes, miss. Excuse me.

Briggs leaves the cell and William Cain enters. He has a bottle of wine, newspapers, a cake and some flowers.

William Celia.

Celia goes to him and kisses his cheek, takes the flowers.

Celia Will?

William Yes. Sorry if it's a . . . I was going to give you some notice and come next week but I thought unannounced might be pleasant.

Celia Yes. Quite. So . . . Are these for me?

William No. They're for the psychopath on the next floor.

Celia It's so sweet of you. Sorry. I'm a bit . . .

William What?

Celia It's just a shock.

William Yes.

Celia Was it difficult to get in?

William I robbed the firm. And a bank.

Celia Yes.

Pause.

William Pinson got me in. The old reptile.

Celia You've brought everything.

Celia scours the front page of a newspaper. Reads:

'Our Prime Minister cannot be blamed for not wanting to give women the vote when it would be in the hands of such hysterics.' Cowards.

William Journalists. Politicians. What do you expect? Drink?

Celia I can't believe you're here.

William You always said I was terribly predictable. Bertram wants to get married.

Celia He told me. Said I was to soften you up about it.

William pours some wine into the mug and raises it to Celia.

William Cheers. (*Taking in the cell.*) Smaller than I imagined.

Celia Did anyone see you come in?

William I didn't climb over the turret. You mean your sisters in arms? You're worried they'll think you're spoilt.

Celia I mustn't have unfair advantages. Access. It's not fair. Do you see?

William I do. I'm a rather brilliant lawyer, not a child. Strange to be in the crucible itself.

Pause.

Celia It feels like a rather private activity.

William You seem more yourself in here than at home.

Celia Really? I can't get used to this at all.

William Do you want me to leave?

Celia No, of course not.

William So what do you think about the two of them?

Celia Bertie seems pretty smitten.

William Her father's a bit of a climber.

Celia As long as they're happy.

William That's enough, do you think?

Celia Don't become middle-aged, Will. Please. I've never asked you for anything.

William walks over to the window and looks out.

William You're very high up, aren't you? One would need a dozen sheets to shimmy down. Those bloody great walls. Christ. (*Pause.*) What?

Celia Nothing.

William sits next to Celia who takes his hand.

So . . . tell me what's happening in the outside world?

William Nothing. Nothing's happening. How is it in here? Any changes?

William looks away distracted, Celia looks at the newspaper.

Celia No. Christ. There's a warning here to telephone girls. Says to be careful about receiving bouquets as men have been drugging them.

William sees Celia's prison books.

William You've some books?

Celia No. They've built a cairn over Captain Scott's grave. Where his tent was.

William Sorry?

Celia They've put a cross on top and planted his skis upright in the ice next to it. It looks strangely religious in the middle of nowhere.

William They were only eleven miles off. One more day and they'd have made it. I think you should see a doctor. When you're released.

Celia Why?

William A psychiatrist.

Celia Do you think I'm mental?

William Not at all. People simply go to Klein for advice. I expect one day it'll be all the rage.

Celia Klein? You've found someone already.

William He was recommended.

Celia So who have you been talking to about your lunatic wife?

William Nobody. Langham was saying his brother's been having treatment since he came back from the Transvaal.

Celia Treatment?

William If nothing else it might be good material for your stories. I want you to be happier is all. It's my birthday.

Celia What? Oh God, Will, I'm sorry. All the days meld into one here.

William You did ask me for something. When you were ten years old. You asked to borrow some of my clothes. So that you could adopt a disguise. And you begged me to run away with you. To Egypt.

Celia Ah. Yes. Well. I was a child then. Everything seemed possible.

William Yes. You were a child. So was I.

SCENE TEN

Hyde Park. Afternoon. Some soapboxes: Florence stands on one. Fellow Suffragettes are near her, including Mrs

*Schliefke, who presides over the singing. A small crowd
has gathered to listen, including Charlie Power, Hunt
and Brown.*

Florence Over a thousand women have been to prison
during the course of this agitation. Last summer there
were one hundred and two suffragettes incarcerated at
one time. Of these ninety were forcibly fed. Some of
them twice a day. Our comrade Kitty Marion has been
force-fed up to two hundred times to date. The last
horrors we witnessed were those of the Boer War.
Women and children starved and died in concentration
camps that British soldiers erected and imposed upon
them. We shouted then about the outrage and we were
heard. We are in peacetime now. Violence is being
inflicted behind secret walls. Upon neither spies nor even
wives of our enemies. But upon our own women.

*Celia and Eve join the women. Celia and Eve light up
cigarettes.*

Hunt How dare you, madam? How dare you compare
yourselves to our men who fought out there!

Florence I was not, sir. But we are soldiers of a sort.

Hunt Men gave their lives! They died that this country
might prosper and that you might be secure!

Florence My point was that no one should be hidden,
gagged or muzzled whether it be in a police cell, a prison
or a refugee camp.

Brown Unnatural they are! And look at that. Smoking
in one of the royal parks. If you was my dog!

Celia Are you addressing me, sir?

Florence Let it never be said that we did not know what
was going on around us. Or that we knew but did not
fight to change it.

Brown Christ. In a minute. Not now but in a minute . . . if you was my dog!

Celia I'm very glad I'm not your dog.

Florence We have been prevented recently from petitioning Parliament. It is every citizen's right to do so. The present Liberal government forces us to be militant! Deeds not words!

Brown I'd do you a deed. I'd do you all a bloody deed.

Celia Do you have healthy relations with your wife, sir?

Brown You bitch! Anarchist socialist bitch!

Hunt Language, sir! This is a public place. And the ladies!

Brown explodes and heads over to Celia to try and hit her.

Brown I'll give them fucking ladies. That's what you want, isn't it, you bitch! Bitches! Unnatural fucking bitches, all of you!

Charlie Power intervenes and tries to keep Brown from Celia.

Charlie Oi! Back off now! Get out of it!

Brown A right fucking servicing is what they want!

Hunt Sir! Stop this now! Stand back!

Florence Sir! Celia! Celia!

There is a messy scuffle. Brown is floored by Charlie.

Charlie Had enough yet, eh?

Brown gets up and runs off.

Brown Piss off, the lot of you!

Hunt We should find a policeman.

Florence You are naive, sir, if you think they'll be helpful to us. No surrender!

Women No surrender!

Charlie (*to Celia*) Do you want a brandy? Shall I get you one?

Celia What? A what?

Charlie For the shock. I work over there at the Ritz.

Celia Thank you, but there's no harm done.

Charlie Sorry about that, ladies. Come over and find me sometime. I'll serve you the best wine and only charge you for house.

Florence Thank you, sir. And good luck to you with getting the vote. No surrender!

Charlie No surrender!

Charlie runs off, amused. Florence goes to her pile of pamphlets and starts to give them out. Eve takes Celia's arm.

Eve Celia.

Celia You kept very quiet.

Eve I didn't know what to . . . I didn't want to . . .

Celia What? Show any vestige of backbone? Come on, let's get a stiff drink.

Celia and Eve leave. Florence watches them. Mrs Schliefke takes the cue for the women to start singing 'The March of the Women'. They sing a few lines from it.

SCENE ELEVEN

Holloway Prison. Eve's cell. Night. A lamp with a gas jet burns in the dark. Eve sits, motionless, on a plank bed. She lies down and tries to settle away from the light. She gets up and goes to the grille in the door. Day five of her strike.

Eve Excuse me. Excuse me!

The sound of footsteps and keys. The Wardress stands outside the cell.

Can you put out the light? I can't sleep with it on.

Wardress You're under observation.

Eve For what?

The Wardress walks away.

For what?

Eve lies on the bed and watches the gas jet, then turns away from it. The flame flickers, Eve sits up. It becomes brighter. She walks to the door.

I can't have the light on! Please! Please!

Eve picks up her shoe from the floor and smashes the glass lamp. A bell sounds. The Wardress and a Guard come in and drag her out of her cell.

SCENE TWELVE

Dr Klein's surgery. Afternoon. Dr Klein sits opposite Celia Cain. Occasionally he refers to notes about her on his desk.

Klein You haven't been sleeping?

Celia No.

Klein Your husband is very worried.

Celia glances at the book on Klein's desk.

It's about Elizabeth the First.

Klein finds the frontispiece with Elizabeth's words. He gives it back to her, Celia reads it.

Celia 'I freeze and yet am burned.'

Klein Do you like history?

Celia It depends whose it is.

Celia refers to her file.

How much of mine is in there?

Klein In your file? You grew up in Hampshire. Married at eighteen. From a large family, your father served in India, your mother lives in Maidenhead.

Celia File is an anagram of life, isn't it? You're an alienist, aren't you? So what would your verdict be to the court so far? That I'm too sane to be locked up or too mad to let roam?

Klein I'm sure you're quite *compos mentis*. But Holloway must take its toll, no?

Celia I've led a privileged life. Prison redresses the balance rather. What else is in there?

Klein You had your first child when you were nineteen. The first of seven.

Celia I don't want to talk about my children.

Klein Why not?

Celia Because they're mine. What do you think of Freud?

Klein I find his attitude towards women is both patronising and irresponsible. You were placed in the hospital ward the last time you were incarcerated?

Celia My window looked out onto the girls in the exercise yard. Two of them were always laughing together. One was about eighteen the other perhaps thirty. The girl's hair kept blowing into her face and eyes and her companion kept brushing it away for her because the girl needed to keep her hands warm in her pockets. The friend understood that.

Klein Is that what you would like? To be understood?

Celia To be loved, you mean?

Klein Is that your definition of understanding?

Celia What I would really like is . . . is a cigarette.

Klein Do you understand your husband?

Celia I'm not supposed to. I'm his wife. We grew up together. I adored him from age eight to eleven. So I suppose we had three good years.

Klein Your husband would like for you to be exempt from conviction if you are ever part of a Suffragette Deputation again.

Celia I'm always part of the Deputation. And if you're part of it then the whole point is to get yourself arrested.

Klein You petition at Parliament?

Celia We endeavour to. And Downing Street.

Klein In which case you'll be arraigned next week. If I pronounce your mind fragile the court will be reluctant to pass sentence, do you see?

Celia And you've discussed this with my husband?

Klein It was more his idea than mine, in point of fact.

Celia So he's not actually worried about my mental health. Just that I shouldn't be incarcerated.

Klein He is concerned that your health will deteriorate inside.

Celia What else?

Klein Nothing else. I'm hoping that you will walk free on Wednesday in which case we should meet on a weekly basis. On a good day I'm terribly perceptive.

Celia And on a bad day?

Klein Nobody sees me on a bad day.

Celia I like this area. Have you practised here long?

Klein The Jews have a very high opinion of themselves.

Celia I'm sorry?

Klein It's a very Jewish area.

Celia You're Jewish, aren't you?

Klein German. I thought about anglicising my name because people often jump to the wrong conclusion.

Celia Except then you'd be Dr Little?

Klein Quite. So. I ask myself, what can we do for this new woman we see before us?

Celia Very little I expect. Goodbye, Klein. I'll see myself out.

Celia stands and exits.

SCENE THIRTEEN

Celia's parlour. Celia and Florence have a pile of leaflets and letters to collate and put into envelopes. Florence is a mini-production line. Celia is slow and stops now to smoke.

Florence You're very distracted today.

Celia I'm going to the prison later. To visit Miss Douglas.

Florence stops and looks at her.

What?

Florence resumes work.

Flo?

Florence I said nothing.

Celia You don't need to.

Florence There are people inside at the moment who you've known a lot longer than that one.

Celia Why do you dislike her?

Florence I don't. You became very close. Very quickly.

Celia I don't think she has many chums.

Florence Where did you put the list and pencil?

Celia vaguely looks for the list and pencil.

Celia She's managed to get herself arrested every time. That's pretty impressive. And she only joined the Union a few months ago.

Florence She should have signed up a lot sooner then, shouldn't she?

Celia She's had no advantages. No education to speak of.

Florence She's not the only factory girl locked up in there. You behave like schoolgirls together. Giggling. Smoking. Always setting up your own little camp at meetings. I don't like people attaching themselves to the cause just because they have nothing else. We're not a headquarters for lost souls.

Celia I'd have thought that was exactly what we were. And I don't call serving seven months' hard labour attaching yourself to the cause. It's hardly the action of a sycophant, is it? What do you want her to do? Nail herself up to the cell wall?

Florence Exactly.

Celia What?

Florence A martyr. She's lonely. And she plays the victim.

Celia She doesn't. Anyway, isn't that the point? That women are victims.

Florence No no no! I can't believe you sometimes.

Celia By our circumstances. I didn't mean victims per se. It's just a word, Florence. Don't react to me like I'm Lord Curzon or the bloody sledgehammer. It's just phraseology. For God's sake, we're both on the same side, aren't we?

Florence She's become addicted to the drama of it all. I tried telling her the history of the movement and she asked me if I'd met any of the famous actresses.

Celia Which is an innocent enough question.

Florence It's not the point though, is it? Why we're here.

Celia You're being very extreme.

Florence Well let's not be extreme, then. Let's not care who's part of the Union or why they've joined. Let's just have a party and sing militant songs, shall we? What the hell are we going to achieve if we're not extreme? And are you ever going to stop smoking that bloody cigarette and help me here?

Celia I'm helping you already. You work faster when you're angry. (*Pause.*) I tell you what, Flo, if things continue to flag here they're dying for you to become part of the Russian Women's Army.

Florence The Battalion of Death? They sound a bit soft.

Celia starts to help.

Oh. She moves.

The women work together.

SCENE FOURTEEN

Holloway Prison. Eve's cell. Dusk. Celia is in civilian clothes; she has a basket of provisions. Eve is in her prison uniform.

Eve I didn't think they let people in.

Celia I'm not people.

Eve Did you have to pay?

Celia No. I walked though the walls. How have you been? I just wondered if there was anything I could do for you out there? Or bring you?

Eve I don't want anything. Why have you come to see me?

Celia You're striking. What day are you on?

Eve Three.

Celia I thought you might want me to take a message to your sister. In Limehouse.

Eve No. Thanks.

Celia takes out parcels from her basket.

Celia I brought you some spring water. And look, so you don't have to use the dog soap. Lemon. Smell.

Eve smells it.

How's your stomach? . . . You'll be out in a month. I miss our working in the kitchen. Those mountains of potatoes. Perverse, isn't it? You're tired. I should let you rest.

Celia leaves the basket for Eve on the floor and prepares to leave.

Eve There's a girl in your cell now. She's fifteen. She didn't stop screaming all night.

Celia You've had no sleep, poor thing. What's she in for?

Eve She smothered her child. They were going to hang her or send her to the asylum. Except her employer has offered to buy her back. He's been raping her since she was eleven. They kicked her out when she started to show and she had the baby months before its time in an alleyway.

Celia Oh. Well, perhaps they won't let him take her back.

Eve They'll let him. Money. Bastard.

Celia Did you ever negotiate them turning out the light for you? There's lavender there too. And newspapers.

And pen and paper. Have you met anyone new? Have you had any nice chats in the kitchen?

Eve Who else are you visiting? Celia?

Celia Nobody. I'm not visiting anybody else.

Eve Why not?

Celia Oh, and books. So you don't have to read prison issue.

Eve Celia.

Celia Yes? . . . My father always said it was a lie if you didn't finish your sentence.

Eve It wasn't a lie.

Celia No.

Eve No. It wasn't a fucking lie.

Celia picks up a prison-issue book.

Celia I wasn't being especially literal. You haven't touched your *How to Maintain a Perfect Household*. Some of the pages aren't even cut.

Eve You laughed. When we were smashing all those windows.

Celia sits herself next to Eve and looks at the book.

Celia Yes.

Eve I've been . . .

Celia What? What have you been? The only really important thing is to be brave. (*Reading the book.*) 'How to remove stubborn stains.'

Celia turns the pages.

Not one wretched sinner has been interested in reading about shining steps or baking the perfect cake.

Eve I'm glad.

Celia That no one wanted to bake to perfection?

Eve That you only came to see me.

Their heads become closer, they turn the pages together.

Celia Yes. Yes, so am I.

They gently move against each other, Eve touches Celia's face, they kiss, gently. Eve breaks away; self-conscious of her breath, she covers her mouth. Celia uncovers it and pulls her back to her. They kiss more strongly. Celia drops the book.

SCENE FIFTEEN

The Cains' parlour. Evening. Celia sits in the dark by a lamp. William walks in, puts down his bag and takes off his gloves. Mrs Collins tends the fire.

William Evening, Mrs Collins.

Mrs Collins Sir. Weather's on the turn.

William It is. (*To Celia.*) How was your day?

Celia It was alright. You look terribly serious.

William I need to ask you something.

Celia Is it to do with your mother?

William No. Nothing to do with Mo. That'll be fine, thank you, Mrs Collins.

Mrs Collins Very good, sir.

Mrs Collins exits. Pause.

Celia What is it?

William How was your work? Did you finish your story?

Celia No. I'm never going to finish it before the next stretch. Florence has gone in again, did I tell you already?

William No.

Celia I forget who I've spoken to. For that policeman in Cannon Street. Five months they gave her when it should be three maximum.

William Really?

Celia She's making a huge stink about the feeding. She's holed herself up with furniture and refuses to come out. She's never done that before.

William And you haven't changed your mind? About the Deputation next month? Or striking in there?

Celia Why would I? Have you been at the Club? Maybe Pinson could put in a word for Flo?

William I'll ask him. Although I suspect she'd rather I didn't.

Celia You're not squiffy already, are you?

William Would you just stop all of this please, Celia? For me.

Celia Stop?

William I don't ask it lightly.

Pause.

Celia You said you'd never ask me to.

William That was before it was dangerous.

Celia First of all you try and pronounce me lunatic. Now you want me to be a no-show.

William Better a no-show than a dead one, don't you think? Who do you actually think you represent?

Celia Half the human race.

William I don't see my mother begging you to lay down your life for her.

Celia I don't think she'd be averse to it.

William You don't represent the whole of womankind.

Celia Because they're institutionalised. Women are prisoners in their own home. They don't even realise it.

William But you do? Thanks.

Celia looks at him. Pause.

I've not asked you to step down before. I've not interfered. In fifteen years. Would you? Please? For me? . . . I see.

Celia Actually you don't. I know when you changed. It was Hyde Park last summer. Ever since then you've tried to accept it but you can't.

William What? What about Hyde Park?

Celia The march. When you saw all our thousands converge. Men don't like to see a convoy of women. It unsexes us.

William Ridiculous.

Celia You're white with anger underneath all your apparent support, aren't you?

William Am I really? I'm going out. Is that permitted? Or is that also up for analysis?

Celia That's all you ever do really, isn't it? Go out. Come home. I suppose there's a routine to it. You leave sober and you return plastered.

William Did you ever think why that might be? Do you know how many evenings you spend furthering the cause?

Celia How many hours do you spend at the law firm?

William As many as I need to in order to support my family.

Celia And getting tight at the Club is another act of altruistic charity you perform for us, is it?

William I go to the Club that I might hear myself think.

Celia Are your blotto thoughts more coherent than your sober ones? Or is it just that they are louder?

William Louder. Stronger. Purer. Funnier. You haven't the slightest inkling of what goes on inside my head. You treat me as though I were stupid.

Celia Well, I don't, actually. I just don't.

William And then you use that tone. That you use at the meetings.

Celia You're acting like a child.

William Why wouldn't I? You preferred me as a child.

William starts to leave.

Celia No, don't walk out. I know you're furious. But we're talking. And we never do. Talk.

William It's rather louder than talk. And I'm not angry. I'm simply tired. Very tired. Don't wait up. You're quite sure about all this? You won't change your mind?

Celia Don't come into my room late. Pissed.

William I haven't done that in a long time. Even animals know when they're not wanted.

William exits.

SCENE SIXTEEN

Holloway. Night time. Florence is in her cell. There are a table and chair barricaded against the door. Guards and Wardresses stand outside. One Guard holds a long rubber hose pipe. Another Guard waits near a faucet.

Guard You're keeping the doctors waiting.

Florence Good. Better for them to wait than to dishonour their profession.

Guard You still refuse to come with us?

Florence I do.

Guard That's prison property you're using. We're coming in.

They start to push the cell door against the barricade of the table and chair. Florence tries to keep the table in place.

Florence I'm a political prisoner, not a lunatic! 'Only be thou brave and . . . only be thou brave . . .'

Guard In!

They force the door in against the table. Florence struggles with them and runs into a corner. The Guards take Florence from her cell into a punishment cell. There is a mess of struggle and people.

Do it, Moyle. Everyone else out!

A Guard comes in with the hose and directs it at Florence. She screams with the pressure and the cold of it, huddles into a ball. The hose is kept on far longer than is needed. Finally Moyle turns it away and another Guard turns it off at the faucet. Florence is

*disorientated, crying. The Guards haul her up and lead
her out of the cell towards the Doctor's office.*

SCENE SEVENTEEN

*Eve's lodgings. Afternoon. Celia and Eve are on Eve's
bed, semi-clothed. There are a couple of empty bottles of
beer. Eve has her head on Celia's lap. The sun streams
onto the floor.*

Celia We should go to France. You'd adore the Parisian
women. They've got the most amazing breasts. What?

Eve I don't want to be around loads of women.

Celia I wasn't inferring that you were a raving bulldyke.
Just that they were lovely. I'm going to buy you a rug.
We can lie on it together. Sunbathe. On your floor.

Eve Don't buy me anything. I don't need anything.

Celia I'm not lying there as it is.

Eve I swept it. This morning.

Celia Doesn't stop you getting splinters in your arse,
does it?

Eve Put a blanket down.

Celia I could have it delivered. And be wrapped up
inside it?

Eve What?

Celia Nothing. I'll get you one. Is there any more beer?

Eve I'll get some.

   Eve starts to get up, Celia stops her.

Celia Would you like a Persian one? Like a flying carpet?

Eve I don't want a fucking rug. What?

Celia When you swear. I like it.

Eve Fucking rug. Fucking Persian fucking woven fucking carpets.

Celia kisses Eve. They embrace.

Eve It's a bit . . . terrifying.

Celia It's not. I promise you it's not.

Eve I just never thought . . . it's like I've been . . .

Celia Waiting.

Eve I wish that I was untouched.

Celia Nobody really touched you.

Eve I'd like to be . . . clean. For you.

Celia I think I love you.

Eve looks away, moves away.

Eve? Eve.

Eve shakes her head.

Darling. Do you want me to go?

Eve shakes her head.

What then? Please.

Eve It's just . . . good. That's good. That you . . .

Celia That I love you.

Eve nods her head, cries.

251

Eve I wish I was . . .

Celia What? What, sweetheart?

Eve I wish I was a virgin who read books.

Eve cries and Celia laughs. Celia holds her.

Celia Angel. Promise me you'll never be a virgin. Especially a bookish one. It's alright. You cry, sweetheart. You cry. I don't want you to be anything. You hear me? Nothing other than what you are. Please.

Eve Yes.

Celia Don't be anything. Just be as you are.

Celia kisses Eve.

Eve Yes.

Celia That is all that I want.

Eve All I want.

Celia All I want.

Blackout.

End of Act One.

Act Two

Epping Forest. Dusk. Eve sits on a tree stump and smokes a cigarette. Celia Cain approaches with a large rifle in hand, pointed at Eve. Eve looks at her.

Celia Smoking. In a public place.

There are several gunshots in the vicinity. Eve looks around at the woods and smiles.

Eve Are you going to shoot me?

Celia I might tie you to a tree. Why aren't you joining in like a good scout?

Eve There weren't enough to go around.

Celia Bloody feeding frenzy. They act like children. Someone'll get fed up with it in a minute. Probably Schliefke. What's the matter?

Eve Just our pretending. Being distant.

Celia Distance can be very alluring.

Celia kisses Eve but breaks from her as she sees women approach: Florence, Mrs Schliefke and other Suffragettes, all with revolvers in hand.

Florence Celia, Miss Douglas, are you with us?

Celia Evidently we are, Flo, else we wouldn't be stood in the middle of Epping Forest, would we?

Florence Miss Beecham, would you lend your revolver to Miss Douglas, please? Let's try for the trees over there. And remember. Cock.

Two of the women giggle. Miss Beecham gives her revolver to Eve.

Ladies. Please.

Suffragette Sorry.

Second Suffragette Sorry.

The women arrange themselves to shoot.

Florence Come then. Pick your targets.

The women aim.

Mrs Schliefke I'm still rather perplexed why Lady Cain has a rifle and we all have revolvers.

Celia Do you want it?

Mrs Schliefke No no. I was merely commenting.

The women aim again silently, carefully. Their attention melds the group into one serious whole.

Florence Now. Fire!

The women shoot in unison.

Good. And again.

They cock and aim their guns.

Fire!

They fire.

Ready . . .

They cock their guns.

Aim.

They aim.

Fire.

They fire.

Good.

Mrs Schliefke Should we not be practising our throwing, Miss Boorman? For tomorrow.

Celia If you can't hit a window at two feet you shouldn't really be on it, Mrs Schliefke.

Mrs Schliefke I'm not saying I can't. Simply that it might be fruitful to rehearse. All I meant about the rifle was that we won't really ever use it, will we?

Florence Preparation is all.

Mrs Schliefke Quite. But my point is . . .

Celia Do you want my big gun, Mrs Schliefke? I give it to you. Here.

Celia takes off her rifle and presents it to Mrs Schliefke, who will not take it.

Mrs Schliefke I don't want it. And actually I rather resent your tone. We're all on the same side after all, aren't we?

Celia Absolutely. It doesn't mean we cease to be individuals though, does it?

Florence takes the rifle.

Florence We've no time for this. Let's get back to the targets . . . Celia?

Celia We'll catch you up.

Florence hesitates.

What? I thought we were snipers, not schoolgirls.

The other women start to walk away, leaving Florence.

Florence It's messy. To divide up like this.

Celia Schliefke says you're on Downing Street next week.

Florence You need to get on with her better.

Celia Why did I hear it from her and not you?

Florence I thought I'd told you.

Celia That's utter rot. You don't listen to a word I say, do you? You need to give your body time to recover.

Florence There is no time, Celia. If we don't keep pushing.

Celia There are thousands have been in and willing to go in again. Your dead bones are good for no one except your dog, Flo. And I'm not looking after that stinking hound if you don't come out alive.

Florence Are you coming?

Celia You're not twenty-one.

Florence And I have no desire to be such an age. All I remember of being twenty-one was crying like a loon. We're lining up the cans now.

Florence walks away.

Eve Does Florence know?

Celia Flo's omniscient. She knows everything.

Eve Do you mind that she knows?

Celia Why would I?

Celia takes Eve's face in her hands, looks at her.

SCENE TWO

A Gentleman's Club. Evening. Grey sits with Seely at one table. Curzon, drunk, sits at another with Cecil. William Cain sits by himself. Men drink, smoke, read the news.

Grey What are you working out?

Seely Controversial Russian composer. Ten letters.

Grey I thought they were all controversial.

Seely Fourth letter 'a'.

Grey What? Why?

Seely Rivers brought it back for me. From America. It's a puzzle. Word-cross.

Grey Word what?

Seely You fill in the white squares and the words going down have to tally with the across letters and words too, do you see?

Seely hands it to Grey.

Grey Bloody stupid. Child's game, surely?

Seely The Yanks are going ga-ga about it.

Grey We've produced a race of bloody infants.

Curzon Stravinsky.

Seely Thank you.

Grey Didn't have you down as a bohemian, Curzon.

Curzon How's that burgundy, Cain?

William It's good.

Curzon And how is your wife?

The other men look towards William and Curzon.

William Quite well.

Curzon Hasn't lost her appetite lately?

William ignores the remark. Curzon pours himself another drink.

Cecil I think you might have had enough, old chap?

Curzon Is the little lady inside or outside at the moment, Cain?

William Where my wife is at this moment is no business of yours, sir.

Curzon Quite. Possibly it's rather difficult to ascertain her whereabouts most of the time?

William Why do you talk out the notion of female suffrage every time it comes up in the House?

Grey I wasn't aware that we did.

William What are you actually scared of?

Grey I'm sorry?

William The first time it was proposed you prioritised a lighting bill. You debated the pros and cons of automobile lamps for hours to prevent any debate about the rights of women.

Curzon Road safety, Cain. Damn important.

William You've torpedoed their bills ever since.

Grey It's not strictly a political matter.

William Then what is it?

Grey Logistics.

William Do you imagine you'll be mentally castrated if you give them a voice?

Curzon Curious that the term should come to you so easily, don't you think? Castrated, what?

Cecil Steady on, Curzon.

Seely Actually I don't think many of our cabinet would notice mental castration. It's more the noise in their private rooms they'd object to.

William And what's your thinking on it?

Seely I prefer to do my thinking at work, not here.

William The last time my wife was in Holloway a woman in the next door cell was heavily pregnant. She finally gave birth. In her cell. In the middle of the night. She had a child.

Curzon What did you expect her to have, a monkey?

William What are you? A man or a puppet?

Curzon You'd know how it feels to be a puppet with a wife like yours, no?

William If you insult my wife once more I shall cuff you.

Curzon If you so much as brush my collar I'll make it my business to have you ejected from Chambers. Chancery. And anywhere you desire to frequent.

Seely Come on, chaps. We're not a load of navvies.

A Waiter approaches with another bottle of wine for William.

Put Mr Cain's bill on our tab, would you?

William No.

William stands and prepares to leave.

Curzon Go on, Cain. Save your money and spend it on your wife. Buy her a square meal. Or a gag.

William approaches Curzon, pulls him and punches him. Curzon reels and falls, covering his head.

Not my head! Please. Please. Not my head.

The gentlemen watch as Cecil goes to Curzon's side and William leaves.

William Go back to your washing, Curzon! Go back to your fucking washing!

SCENE THREE

The Prison. Florence's cell. Night. Briggs stands at the door.

Florence Why does he want to see me?

Briggs does not reply.

Are you silent because you're not interested or is it a tactic to terrify me?

Briggs Trouble.

Florence nods. Dr Vale comes in with notes in his hand.

Vale Miss Boorman.

Florence Yes.

Vale Dr Vale.

Florence I know who you are. How many unwilling mouths did you feed today?

Vale It's my day off, actually.

Pause. Vale looks at the walls of the cell.

Did you write this? It's from the Bible.

Florence It's for those who come in after me. To lift their spirits. This is a strange way for you to spend your time off.

Vale It's been bothering me. The treatment. Usually with new procedure one becomes easier with it as time goes on. This time I've felt the reverse. To see women emaciated. Terrified.

Florence You should write to the papers. Tell them how it is.

Vale I'm a general practitioner, not a journalist. And there's been more than enough of all that.

Florence So what do you want with me? This isn't a confessional box.

Vale They said I might speak to you.

Florence And you've spoken.

Dr Vale sits down.

Did you wish to become a doctor when you were a child?

Vale It was expected of me. Yes. I did want to. How is your mouth?

Florence I can speak. That's all that matters to me.

Vale You lost three teeth. The last time you underwent forcible feeding.

Florence I did not lose them, sir. They were not mislaid. They were smashed. By the steel gag that they used to force my mouth open.

Vale Any pain since?

Florence None to speak of.

Dr Vale stands up, walks to the window.

Vale Some of your women on the outside attacked one of our doctors, you know? In an alleyway. Last week, on his way home from here. They whipped him with a riding crop. What do you say to that?

Florence I hope he paid them the going rate.

Vale My wife has no sympathy with the movement.

Florence Would you like me to visit her when I'm out? Is that what this is about?

Vale You have influence here. You're the most senior suffragette who goes on strike.

Florence Yes.

Vale Your people planted another bomb in a railway station. They burn down houses. I can't see why you've reverted to such low tactics when you were starting to gain ground.

Florence We've been gaining ground for years. It becomes more tiring than encouraging in the end. One step forward, two steps back. We ask for very little. Simply to be represented. Taxation without representation amounts to tyranny, don't you think?

Vale How is your heart?

Florence Are you asking me if I'm in love?

Vale If it's weak you must abstain from striking.

No reply.

You're shouted at. Spat upon. Subjected to violence. Why do you do it?

Florence It's what I call life, Doctor. Life.

Vale The younger girls. Some of them will not be able to bear children if they continue to abuse their bodies in this way.

Florence We all have to make sacrifices.

Vale But theirs may be larger than yours.

Florence That is their choice.

Vale Your sister died whilst you were serving time here last autumn. You asked to go to both her sickbed and funeral. You were denied both appeals. That must have been harsh. You were teachers in the same school, weren't you?

Florence finds it hard to speak.

Florence Don't.

Vale Don't . . . what?

Florence I prefer not to.

Vale I've upset you? I'm sorry.

Florence I want to be alone now.

Vale Consider. What I've said to you. Will you?

Florence No. The doctor before you said he would make a mental and physical wreck of me if I continued to strike. Is that humane?

Vale I've given you my time. My care. I'm sorry that you won't listen.

Vale leaves.

Florence (*to herself*) 'Only be thou strong and very courageous. Only be thou strong and very courageous.'

SCENE FOUR

*A park at night. Celia and Eve are up against a back wall,
kissing. They are in a hidden spot but are still vaguely on
guard against passers by. Still they are more involved
with each other than anything else. The sound of a police
bell. Celia breaks away. They sit on a bench together. Eve
rolls a cigarette, she breathes deep. Celia smiles at her.*

Celia Cold?

Eve No.

Celia Good.

Eve What?

Celia laughs.

What?

*Celia shakes her head. They look at each other and
smile and it becomes a laugh. Eve kisses Celia. They
are both aware of the danger but can't stop. A dog
barks. They part slowly.*

Eve Dog. There's foxes behind my block. You got foxes
near you?

Celia No.

Eve I listen to them at night. They always sound like
they're in such fucking pain when they're doing it. I used
to cry. Listening to them. The other night I didn't. First
time.

Celia Will you make me one?

Eve I'll get you a cigarette case. Then you'll always have
some in reserve.

Eve gives Celia her cigarette. Celia tries to light it,

*fails. Eve cups her hands around the light, Celia cups
her hands, the cigarette doesn't light, they start to kiss
each other's hands and mouth, the cigarette forgotten.*

Celia Thank you.

Eve I keep thinking I'll try to be more restrained when
I see you next. Sophisticated. But I never am.

Celia I wouldn't want you to be.

*Celia takes Eve's hand. Eve takes Celia's hand with
both of her hands. Celia takes her hand away and
puts it under Eve's skirts.*

Is that sophisticated?

Eve It's beautiful. Beautiful.

Celia Good.

*They laugh. They kiss gently then sit with their heads
together.*

Eve Do you see the really bright one?

Celia It's Venus. Ishtar.

Eve I keep thinking about your body. I'll be walking
down the street or stacking shelves and I'm smiling like
a bloody madwoman. People think I've been turned by
prison. I make noises and I don't know I'm doing it. I'm
mentally stripping you all the time. I never wanted to see
anyone's body before.

Celia Not even Mr Blair's?

Eve Don't joke about that.

Celia Can you roll me a thinner cigarette please, sweet?

Eve He always wanted the lamp turned up full. He said
he wanted to see the things I was doing to him and that
I should see them too.

Celia Bastard.

Eve My fault. Should have got out.

Celia You were fifteen.

Eve Old enough. I wasn't a child. I felt nausea. Just the sight of his shoulders, fat fucking freckled shoulders.

Celia takes her hand away from Eve's petticoats. Eve takes Celia's hand.

I never thought I minded about all of that. No broken bones. No baby. Since I've known you I've minded. A lot.

Celia You're perfect. You're not damaged.

Eve Not damaged, no. I'm not a machine.

Celia You've got an incredible golden triangle right in the middle of your iris. Will I see you tomorrow?

Eve I'm meant to be doing a night shift.

Celia Tuesday, then?

Eve Tomorrow's fine. Perfect. Are you scared?

Celia I quite like to be scared. It's when I'm not that I start to worry.

Eve What do you mean?

Celia When the dust starts to settle.

Eve What do you mean about the dust settling?

Celia When things become familiar. Lazy.

Eve With your husband?

Celia With him as well.

Pause.

What?

Eve You haven't done this before. You said you hadn't.

Celia Because I haven't. With a woman. I've had affairs, darling. Just a few.

Eve Oh.

Pause.

Celia Oh, sweetheart. You look all hurt. It makes no difference to you, does it?

Eve What?

Celia We've neither of us been lily-white. What's happening is about us now not who's touched us or where in the past.

Celia strokes Eve's hair.

I haven't shocked you, have I? In the park. In the dark. You're sat with a posh floozy.

Pause.

You're surprised. And repelled.

Eve Surprised.

Celia And repelled.

Eve I'm not repelled.

Celia You're a bad liar. You'd never make a poker player.

Eve I don't want to be a poker player.

Celia Kiss me. (*Pause.*) Don't be so bloody conventional. I'm the same person now as I was three minutes ago.

Eve I know. I didn't say you weren't.

Celia Stop looking so beautifully judgemental then.

Eve kisses her; something has shifted a little.

267

Eve We'd better go. Don't want to get locked in.

Celia No. No. We absolutely don't want to get locked in.

They stand and walk out of the park.

SCENE FIVE

The Cains' parlour. Night. Celia sits, reading. William walks in, drunk.

William Books, is it?

Celia You're drunk?

William That's pretty obvious, isn't it? Why ask it like a question when in fact it's a comment. A judgement.

Celia Shall I ring for Hughes? He could make you some tea.

William I want no tea.

Celia Don't.

William Don't what? What am I not to do now?

Celia I'm going up. I'll see you in the morning.

William Inevitably. Are you aware that you stare into space more and more? It's like you've always desired a way to escape from it all. To defect. From the everyday routine. And you've finally found it. Some sort of transcendental something.

Celia I wasn't conscious of it. You must tell me when I do it again.

William Must I? There are many things you're not aware of. Go. Climb into that huge bed of yours.

Celia Have something to eat. Before you go to sleep.

William I don't want to eat.

Celia You'll feel better for it.

William That's rich. Coming from you. Bloody death camp. Where's my pipe? Where have they put it? If you refuse to eat in there. When you come out. There will be no home for you here.

Celia What?

William I may be tight but I'm in earnest.

> *William produces a written statement which he gives to Celia, who reads it.*

Celia This is an ultimatum, is it? How long is my exile to last?

William You can stay with your mother. Live with your mother.

Celia You'd actually witness that? Me? And mother?

William I don't want you to leave our home. Neither do I want you to be butchered by a load of prison doctors. You seem to exhibit no sense of self-preservation whatsoever, consequence of which I am enforcing this condition. I concede that this might be a facile approach to what is loosely termed as protecting one's wife but that is in fact what I'm trying to do.

Celia And you'd cut me off. No home. No money.

William Yes. Exactly.

Celia If you had a sense of humour I'd think this were a joke.

William I have a brilliant sense of humour. It simply eludes you.

Celia William?

William Yes. (*Pause.*) What? Will you step down?

Celia No.

William There we are, then.

Celia I have borne you children. (*Pause.*) Seven children.

William Yes. I know you say I don't notice things, but that fact hadn't escaped my attention.

Celia And we have five children now.

William We do. What is your point?

Celia shakes her head.

I'm sorry.

Celia You're prepared to disown me, abandon me.

William Why do you always have to be so bloody melodramatic? This is Euston, not Sweden. I'm not forcing you into anything. What are you having?

William walks towards the drinks tray.

Celia I want a choice.

William Well, there's brandy or sherry or a pink gin.

William pours himself a drink.

I don't actually see why I should be ashamed or apologetic. I think it's all gone too far. That's simple enough, isn't it? I find the idea of women enduring torture obscene. And a young woman crumpled underfoot at the Derby repugnant. Unnecessary and sensationalist.

Celia You have no idea what it feels like. To be invisible.

William You all seem pretty bloody visible to me.

Celia You don't know.

William So tell me.

Celia You're asking me to tell you after more than twenty years together?

William Yes.

Celia You're drunk.

William Absolutely. I'm an inebriated brute. Without imagination. And of course utterly devoid of sensitivity. Go now. Close your bedroom door and pretend I'm a filthy figment of your imagination.

Celia William.

William And when you hear me crash into my room just pretend it's a beast, a friendly beast, exploring the life of bourgeois suburbia. It's quite normal. No need to be alarmed.

Celia Remember to put out the lights.

William You never cared for it, did you?

No reply.

I felt your cold sweat of relief every time it was done. I felt you reclaim yourself. Every time you pulled the sheets around you. And I heard you. Weeping. You put all your bodily effort into keeping your tears silent. So much so that I didn't dare turn around and ask you what was wrong. Or, perish the thought, try to touch you again. Sorry. I'm a beast. We're all beasts. Goodnight, Beauty. Go on. Piss off and leave me to my self-indulgence. 'Remember me at my best, Pip!'

Celia I will. I do.

William I do. I do I do I do I do. But you don't, do you?

*Celia leaves. William goes to the drinks tray and
pours himself another drink. He starts to walk
towards a chair but stops and crouches down, settles
on the floor. He gets up and goes to the gramophone,
winds it up and puts the needle on the record. 'Oh
You Beautiful Doll' plays, William sits and listens, he
throws his glass at the wall.*

SCENE SIX

*Holloway Prison. The bath house. Evening. A line of
women including Florence, virtually stripped, wait to
enter several cowshed-type baths. A few of the women
have small ragged towels with which they try to cover
themselves. As women come out from behind the bath
doors Briggs throws powder over them. They step on
a scale where a Wardress records their weight and gives
them a large clean handkerchief. There is a basket of
random underclothes that the women then head for and
huddle in a corner to get dressed in. Florence is almost
naked, waiting to enter the bath. A Young Suffragette
offers her towel to her. Mrs Briggs shouts.*

Briggs Back! Back! Take it back!

Young Suffragette I don't need it. I . . .

Briggs Don't talk! Take it! Now!

Florence Who are you, Briggs?

Briggs No talking.

Florence No. Really. Who are you? How will you
remember yourself when you're old? When you think
of yourself as a young woman? Is this it?

Briggs I'll report you.

Florence I can't explain it to you, can I?

Briggs Quiet. Now.

Florence You should cherish your youth. When it's gone it's gone.

Florence gives the towel back to the Young Suffragette.

Thank you.

Briggs throws a towel towards Florence.

Briggs Pick it up then and no more talking.

Florence does not pick up the towel.

You're heading for isolation, you are. On your own.

The Young Suffragette picks up the towel and offers it to Florence, who does not take it, so the Young Suffragette gives it back to Briggs.

Florence You're a child, Sarah.

Briggs Briggs!

Florence I feel sorry for you.

Briggs I'm not a child. You're the one that's locked up in here. Not me.

Florence The walls are incidental. I'm a child too. I never said I wasn't. Just an older one. I'm going to have my bath now, then you can chuck that powder over me as if I were newborn.

Briggs Just don't talk, that's all.

Florence No. Absolutely. No.

Florence disappears into the bath shed. The other women look at Briggs.

SCENE SEVEN

A tea shop. Dusk. Celia and Eve sit together. Celia looks at the menu. Other couples are at various tables, including Mrs Major and her niece Felicity.

Celia I just think this once I should stand down. He's about to throw me out.

Eve I see that.

Celia Do you think I'm being awful?

Eve No.

Celia You could bunk off too.

Eve No. I got you something.

Eve puts a small gift on the table.

Celia You mustn't spend your money. Bugger. Could you move to the left a little. I've just seen Mrs Major. I can't bear the thought of saying hello. Don't look.

Eve glances over her shoulder then shuffles to her left.

Ta. Do you need some cash?

Eve What? No. Why?

Celia What? I don't see why you're prepared to do the most intimate things with me but as soon as I mention money you take umbrage.

Eve You'd probably take umbrage too, if it was the other way around.

Celia Do you know what the phrase means?

Eve What?

Celia Nothing. Let's open this.

The Waitress approaches.

Waitress Can I take your order, ladies?

Celia Could you give us a moment please? One slow minute?

Waitress Of course, miss. Is it your birthday?

Celia No – I don't have birthdays any more.

The Waitress smiles with Celia and leaves them.

Celia She called me 'miss'. How delicious. Charming uniforms, aren't they?

Eve looks away.

What? Oh, come on.

Celia unwraps the present. It is a cigarette case.

That's just beautiful. Thank you. Really. It's lovely. I've offended you.

Eve It wasn't the money. You just sounded . . . cold.

Celia I find a little coolness helps to put things in perspective.

Eve What? What do we need to put into perspective?

Celia Let's not ask the whole of the tea room, shall we?

Eve I thought you didn't care what other people thought.

Celia There's a time and a place.

Eve So where's ours? Our time. Our place. What's happening, Celia?

Celia Nothing. You've shifted.

Eve I haven't. Why do you say that?

Celia No. Your position darling. Left. Just a smidgen.

Eve stops, shifts her chair a little.

We're simply evolving.

Eve Can't we stay as we were?

Celia We can't remain as primitives, can we? Maybe it's your namesake. You hanker back to an age of innocence. It's quite a strange name to give a child, isn't it? When you think of what she did?

Eve My mother liked it.

Celia Ah yes, your mother. Well, that doesn't surprise me. Everyone's so beastly about poor Eve. I bet the garden would have become pretty dull if she hadn't rebelled. The two of them would have ended up bashing each other's skulls in with a spade if she hadn't transgressed. They'd have suffered irreparable brain damage. Then reeled around digging little burial pits for each other while they lost their minds.

The Waitress approaches.

Waitress Are you ready, miss?

Celia Yes. (*To Eve.*) Yes? We'd like two pots of tea and some sponge fingers, and do you have any *crème brûlée*?

Waitress Yes, miss.

Celia Splendid. All of that then. Times two. Like the ark.

The Waitress exits.

People lose their terror don't they? Once they've touched the area in between each other's legs. Love is just fear, I suppose. Masquerading as a fever. Then you explore each other and suddenly you have licence to become totally pedestrian. And ultimately abusive.

Eve Why are you saying this?

Celia (*indicating a couple at another table*) Look at those two. You'd think deciding what to eat or how much to tip the waiter was as important as the Rights of Man. It's a liquefied co-dependence. An amorphous mentality. Such a waste.

Eve We're not like that.

Celia Not yet.

Eve Why don't you just say if you don't want it?

Celia 'It' being what?

No reply.

If the 'it' is sexual relations with you then yes, I want it. If the 'it' is hiding and feeling perpetually frustrated then no, I don't want it.

Eve I'm in love with you.

Celia No. The reverence has gone. It's not something to mourn. It's rather liberating. Not to be worried about every pose you strike and every expression you make.

Eve It would be different if we were allowed to be together.

Celia Men and women are allowed to be together. And they're the worst of the lot.

No reply.

I risk everything here, Eve. We are in very different positions.

Eve I know. I know that.

Celia You'll be in Holloway within the week. For God knows how long.

Eve What do you want to say?

Celia I think it's better to part sooner than later.

Mrs Major approaches their table with a young niece, Felicity.

Mrs Major Lady Cain! I saw you! How are you? And the children? This is my niece Felicity. Deborah's gal.

Celia Oh, how marvellous. Hello, Felicity. This is Miss Douglas. Mrs Major, Felicity.

Mrs Major I heard about your son, how jolly, and they've chosen a perfect duck of a house, haven't they?

Celia They have.

Mrs Major (*to Eve*) You're wearing the badge! Good for you. Were you in for very long?

Eve shakes her head.

Good. Good. Well, we won't keep you. So pleasant, though. Do give my best to your family. Goodbye.

Celia Goodbye. Love to Dodo. Goodbye, Felicity.

Felicity Goodbye.

They exit. Celia looks at Eve. Pause.

Eve You said . . . part. Be apart.

Celia I don't want to waste your time. Or break your heart.

Eve Is that a line from one of your stories?

Celia Not yet, no.

Eve You sound like you rehearsed this.

Celia Important things should be rehearsed.

Celia pushes the cigarette case towards Eve.

Take this, darling. You use it. I'd prefer you to keep it.

Eve You think I'd use it? You've very little imagination for a writer. You should go. I feel like I'll say something awful.

Celia Say it. Please. You'll feel better if you say it.

Eve You'll feel better if I say it.

Celia Please.

Eve shakes her head.

I'm sorry if this has all been awkward. I'm rather a beginner, as you know.

Eve gets up and walks out. The Waitress comes over with cakes. Celia lights a cigarette, puts some money on the table and leaves.

SCENE EIGHT

A bedroom in the Ritz. Charlie stands by the window drinking wine. Celia sits, drinking. She lights a cigarette but does not smoke it. There is an empty wine bottle and a half-full one.

Charlie Looks beautiful from up here. The park. The lights. Don't it? How come you're staying here tonight?

Celia I've helped myself to your cigarettes. Do you mind?

Charlie Is this what you New Women do, is it?

Celia Stay in expensive hotels?

Charlie Invite the staff up? Is that your contribution towards democracy, is it?

Celia Do you like working here?

Charlie It has its moments. What sort of books do you write?

Celia Ghost stories.

Charlie No? Really? I've got an idea I always wanted to do. About a man in the fog. The streets he goes down. People he meets. Then he becomes the fog, he's in it and he becomes it.

Celia Are you drunk?

Charlie I'm intoxicated. By you.

Charlie inhales on his cigarette then lets the smoke out slowly.

Celia You're like a dragon.

Charlie I am a dragon. I've got great big teeth. And a giant tail. Why can't you go home, then? What did you do?

Celia I just can't.

Charlie Why did you invite me up here?

Celia Because you have a constant supply of cigarettes.

Charlie Can I sit next to you?

Celia I won't bite.

Charlie That's a shame. Sorry. I'm terrible. Have you done this before?

No reply. Charlie sits down next to Celia.

Can I just? To illustrate something?

He indicates his hand to her hip. Celia does not stop him.

Look at that.

He places his hand on her hip, then slowly follows the line to her thigh.

That curve there. And this one here. It's beautiful. Men are all straight lines. Angular. Like dead bodies already. Women. Look. You got this bit. And that. I can't imagine you laid out on a slab. Whereas I look halfway there. You gonna smoke that?

Charlie takes the cigarette from Celia and kisses her.

Celia No. Don't.

Charlie I thought this was what you wanted.

Celia No.

Charlie What then?

Celia I thought we might talk. About things.

Charlie Oh. What do you want to talk about?

Celia Anything.

Charlie Football?

Charlie stands up and moves away.

Celia I'm sorry. I'm confusing you.

Charlie You're very beautiful. I always thought that. When I saw you speak with your lot. In the park. Would you like me to leave?

Celia Thank you. For being a gentleman.

Charlie I'm not being a gentleman inside my head.

Celia I'm very lucky, aren't I? You might have been a brute.

Charlie How do you know I'm not?

Celia You liked the pictures on the stairwell.

Charlie Christ. You really know how to look after yourself, don't you?

Celia I had a bust up with my friend. She's . . . it's rather affected me.

Charlie You want some more Chablis?

Celia Please. She's rather cut up about it.

Charlie gets up, pours two glasses of wine and gives one to Celia.

Charlie Is she sick?

Celia Sick?

Charlie You're worried about her?

Celia Yes. I am. I'm all torn up.

Charlie Here's to you. Poor thing. Poor girl. You're in a bit of a state, aren't you?

He puts his arm around Celia.

Celia I don't really know what I'm doing.

Charlie Course you don't. That's alright.

He kisses her gently. Celia responds. Charlie caresses her.

Celia Yes.

Celia gives in to his embrace.

Charlie You're a right tart, aren't you?

Celia Yes. Possibly. Am I?

Charlie You don't know whether you're coming or going, do you? You won't even remember this tomorrow, will you?

Celia No. No, I hope not.

Charlie puts his hand up her skirts and negotiates the layers of underwear until he has passed them. Celia flinches.

Charlie Does that hurt?

Celia Yes.

Charlie Nice?

Celia No.

Charlie No?

Celia Really. Please. Don't.

Charlie I thought you'd like that.

Celia No.

Charlie Is that a real no or a pretend?

Celia Real.

Charlie takes his hand out from under her skirts.

Charlie I always wondered about women like you. What you'd be like underneath. You all smell the same.

Celia You should go now. Please. I think I'm going to puke.

Celia gets up and exits the room.

Charlie I'll wait for you. Make sure you're alright. Wait a bit. I'll make you better.

Charlie lights a cigarette.

SCENE NINE

Holloway Prison. An office. Morning. Celia and Eve sit on chairs. Celia is in smart civilian clothes, Eve is in her prison uniform.

Eve I don't want to feel this intensely ever again.

Celia Of course you do. And you will. You're young.

Eve I was never young.

Celia Why were you in isolation? Why?

No reply.

I brought you some cigarettes. I've been worried about you. Do you think we might get through this as friends?

Eve lights a cigarette.

Eve You've enough friends as it is.

Celia I don't, as it happens. Not real ones. I rather pretend to be more robust and popular than I really am. It snowed yesterday. Did you see it? I walked through the park and it was catching the sunshine as it fell. Strange how beauty moves one so easily, so visibly, yet one's so trapped when it comes to real emotions. I won't stay. It's not fair that I descend on you like this. A captive audience. I just wanted to see if I could bring you anything? . . . No. Goodbye.

Celia kisses Eve's cheek.

Eve I painted your name on the wall. With blood. I'd been striking for five days and it seemed like the thing to do.

Celia Blood? What blood?

Eve My blood. They stripped me. Looking for the cut. I feel bereft. Shabby.

Celia Well, you're not. Either of those things.

Celia picks up a prison-issue book then drops it to the floor.

Eve You could always write a story, 'Love among the Inverts'.

Celia Don't use that word. It's repulsive.

Eve 'Love'?

Celia I didn't ask you to fall in love with me. I actually warned you against it.

Eve True. Certain movements, signs, you made, could be interpreted as an invitation. If I could take one step away I could protect myself.

Celia I'll protect you.

Pause.

Eve You having a big Christmas?

Celia Florence and I are doing a bash at the Bow Canteen. Presents for all the children.

Eve You said our time together was interesting.

Celia Is that a crime, to find something interesting?

Eve Made it sound a bit like an experiment.

Celia I obviously can't say anything right. I should go.

Eve I'd like to write to you.

Celia You don't need to write to me.

Eve I know I don't need to. I'd like to.

Celia I'm not sure I'm in the right state of mind to receive a letter from you.

Eve Will you leave me your address?

Celia Just send it to the Union.

Eve You know my address. We were . . . together. Many times. In Limehouse. And you won't tell me where you live?

Celia Can I kiss you?

Eve looks away.

I imagined you might not live by the rules. But I think you do as much as the next person.

Eve Who is the next person?

Celia Desire is very strange. One shouldn't try to pin it down.

Eve I thought I heard you. Last week. I was at home. In bed. Late. I couldn't sleep. I was nervous. Foxes were barking. And I heard a woman singing in the square. And I thought you'd come back. That you were stood, down there on the pavement. Singing. I wanted to look out the window, but I didn't dare in case it wasn't you. Then the song stopped. And it was quiet. I thought you were waiting. That you'd shout something up to me. For me to run down to you. Then I jumped up and I looked out and there was no one there. Empty street. Yellow street lamp. Just some laughing round the corner and a bottle being smashed.

Celia I'm sorry I didn't come and sing to you.

Eve goes to the office door and shouts:

Eve Briggs? Can I go back to my cell now, please?

The door is opened and Eve walks out.

SCENE TEN

Holloway Prison. A doctor's office. Morning. An armchair. A Wardress and a Nurse attend while a Guard escorts Eve into the room. There are a few other Guards present. Eve is led to a weighing machine which she stands on, then gets off. A Guard records her weight. Dr Vale greets her.

Vale Morning. Do sit down.

Eve sits.

Where's the sheet?

Nurse Sorry, Doctor.

The Nurse lays down a white sheet under the chair Eve sits down on. Vale listens to her heartbeat with a stethoscope.

Vale How's your heart?

Eve Alright.

Vale Any other problems?

Eve No.

Vale refers to a blue piece of paper from his pocket.

Vale It says here that you are not to be released, even on medical grounds. That you insist on refraining from food?

Eve Yes.

Vale Then I must compel you to take it.

Eve You've got to prove that I'm mad. You're not allowed to perform any operation without a patient's consent.

Vale bows.

Vale These are my instructions.

The Nurse approaches with a long red rubber tube attached to a funnel and a jug of liquid.

Nurse Excuse me, sir, Nurse Beaty is off today so I'm doing it instead. I've not been on before.

Vale The complications are invariably at my end, not yours. You've got about a pint there. You just watch that it's going down and let me know when it's finished, yes?

Nurse Yes sir. Thank you.

The Nurse stands on a chair to hold the apparatus, basically a funnel and a jug of liquid, while the Wardress and Guards stand at Eve's side. Vale prepares himself with a large apron and instruments.

Eve What's in it? What are you putting in me?

Vale Egg and brandy.

Eve I don't want it. I don't like it.

Vale This is not an hotel. If you don't want the stuff, you must simply resume eating. Right. Let's be having you. Don't start pouring until I give the say so, Nurse. And let me know when it's all gone, yes?

Nurse Yes, Doctor.

Wardress Do you want the gag, sir?

Vale No. Let her take it through the nose.

Vale pushes a tube into and up her nose. Eve bodily flinches and the Guards and Wardress hold her down. She is in severe pain, and trying to contain it, but her body is in spasms as Vale feeds it in and talks to the Nurse.

Come on. In you go. Come on. There. Have to push it
in a good twenty inches, you see, Parker, so it goes right
through to the stomach.

Nurse I see.

Vale You can start pouring now.

Nurse Yes sir.

The Nurse watches but does not pour the mixture.

Vale Yes?

She starts to pour, very slowly.

That's it. If ever you're on this end and it's not going
down, you simply pinch the nose, yes? Is it going down?

Nurse Yes sir. Seems to be.

Vale Good. Good.

*Eve's body shakes with the pain and she almost
retches.*

Gag. Get me the wooden gag.

*The Wardress hands him the gag, which he forces into
Eve's mouth. Eve spits it out and struggles.*

Pass me the steel one. You, Parker, keep it there, tight,
would you? Come on now. There's a good girl.

*The Wardress passes Vale the steel gag, who gives it to
Parker to hold steady in Eve's mouth. Eve heaves and
chokes. They wait for one minute for all the liquid to
go down. During this time Eve reaches different
thresholds of pain.*

Nurse It's gone, sir.

Vale Good. Well done. Now we just have to get the
blasted thing out. Gently does it.

The Guard removes the gag. Vale gradually pulls the tube out slowly, which causes more pain than inserting it. Eve writhes and then stops, spent with pain. She lies motionless.

All done. Sit up now when you're ready. All yours, ladies.

Wardress Yes, sir.

The Wardress fetches a basin of water and starts to sponge Eve's chin and face. Vale bends in to look at Eve, who retches over him. He slaps her face.

Vale Stubborn. You must not be so stubborn.

Vale walks out, followed by Parker. The Wardress washes Eve's face then sprinkles her with some eau de cologne. The Nurse remains on the chair.

Wardress You can get down now.

The Nurse does not get down. The Wardress helps Eve to sit up. The Guard helps her gradually to stand.

Guard Do you want to stay put for a bit, girl? Before we go back? To pull yourself together?

Eve shakes her head, almost drugged by the pain. Eve takes his arm and the Wardress takes her other arm. Eve looks beaten, worn, but also like a child, vulnerable. She nods her head and they start to walk together out of the office.

SCENE ELEVEN

Celia's parlour. Dusk. Celia is looking in drawers. William walks in.

William Where have you been?

Celia I stayed with a friend.

William We've all been worried bloody sick.
Telephoning the police station. Hospitals.

Celia Sorry. I can't find my spectacles.

William Is that it? 'Sorry'?

Celia You don't think Liza would have put them in my
room, do you? Please don't go into the sulks. I've rather
had enough of all that.

William I thought you might be dead.

Celia I probably was.

William Could you just for once not speak in code?

Celia I wanted to have one night of my life unaccounted
for. Is that clear enough? Is that permissible? Just a few
hours where nobody knew where I was. I thought it
might be a little like Heaven. Being anonymous for a
moment. Actually it wasn't very pleasant. And I was the
loneliest I've ever felt. Do you feel any better now?
Knowing that my selfish oblivion was actually
repugnant? You're about to throw me onto the streets. I
would have thought my behaviour was pretty typical
under the circumstances.

William Who were you with last night?

Celia I already told you. Do you want names?
Addresses?

William Christ, you're selfish.

Celia I think we've covered this ground before, haven't
we?

William It's not clever. To hurt people. I don't know why
you're scouring my desk. They won't be in there.

Celia picks up a photograph.

Celia I didn't realise you were so sentimental. What's this one called? 'Wife, Pre-Conversion'?

William Don't maul my stuff, thanks.

Celia picks up another photograph.

Celia God. Us on the boat. On your tenth birthday. Coming back from Calais. In that storm. I was terribly sick, wasn't I? Retching over the side.

William Where did you stay?

Celia You held my hair away from my face.

William Where were you?

Celia At the Ritz.

William I just don't understand why you want to make me worry.

Celia Nor do I, Will. Nor do I. I'm sorry. That you worried. I'm sorry.

William Are you drunk?

Celia It depends how long the effects last. You should be able to answer that one. I've not had a drink this morning, if that's what you're asking.

William Why the bloody Ritz, for Christ's sake?

Celia I fancied a view of the park. I thought you'd know it was just me swanning off. One of my gestures.

William I'm not Houdini.

Celia I think he escapes rather than reads minds.

William How was breakfast there? Is it all it's cracked up to be?

Celia It was very good. I watched the soldiers riding, saw the red of their uniforms flash through the trees.

From my window. Very early. Beautiful huge black horses. And they were just running everywhere. It was so wonderful to see them not in formation. I'd forgotten they could be like that. Dust flying up and their swords kept catching the first of the winter sunshine. I felt I might run out there and become part of a tragedy.

William I'm sorry it hasn't been all you hoped for.

Celia I can't change.

William No, of course you can't. It's a ridiculous notion. But I can't climb the walls, you see? So I'm redundant. Those bloody great big grey stones. I'm not attacking you. You simply have no notion, do you? Of how that feels.

Celia You seem different.

William Do I? No. I'm the same.

Celia I have tried. To make a good marriage. I just don't really know how.

William I worry. I do worry. About you.

William breaks down. Celia holds him.

SCENE TWELVE

Eve's lodgings. Late afternoon. There is a white enamel basin of water on the floor. Eve is in her Sunday dress. She takes it off. Then sponges herself clean. She puts the Sunday dress on the floor with the basin in front of her. She picks up the dress and holds it as if it were a person, then puts it down. She crouches by the basin, picks up a cut-throat razor that is next to it. She puts her hands into the basin, cuts her wrists, blood fills the water.

SCENE THIRTEEN

*Holloway Prison. The hospital. Afternoon. Women lie in
hospital beds. Eve is in bed, her wrists bandaged.
Florence enters with a basket of provisions and the
Suffragette magazine. She approaches the Nurse near to
Eve.*

Florence Briggs said I could come in for a short while.
For Miss Douglas.

Nurse Bed number three. Five minutes.

Florence sits by Eve's bedside.

Florence It's me. Florence Boorman. Don't move. Just . . .
What can I get for you? Water? Anything?

Eve Nothing, Miss Boorman.

Florence Florence. So . . . we'll just sit, then. Time will
help. It does. Believe me. The hospital ward's as
bureaucratic as ever, eh? And one young nurse didn't
know what the Union was. I shall tell her before I leave.
Celia's not here?

Eve Gone. To get some tea.

Florence Good. Tea is always good.

Eve How's your motor car?

Florence Splendid. Yes, it's splendid. Thank you.

Eve Sorry. I'm very sorry.

*Florence takes Eve's hand. They are silent together.
Celia enters with two cups of tea.*

Celia Flo. Thanks for coming. I'd have got you a cup.
Have mine.

Florence No no. Well, Miss Douglas is looking just fine, isn't she?

Celia I've seen you look better. I'm only allowed another few minutes, Flo.

Florence I only came to collect you and to say hello to the wounded soldier. I've brought some things. There's *The Suffragette*.

She takes the Suffragette *magazine out of her basket.*

Perhaps I'll give that to the nurse, shall I? I'll wait by the gate. Goodbye, Eve.

Celia Thanks, Flo.

Eve Night.

Florence leaves.

Celia It's not night, sweetheart. It's day. Can you see that?

Eve Mm.

Celia Can you see my hand? It's not dark.

Celia puts her hand near to Eve's face. Eve takes Celia's hand and puts it against her cheek. Celia sits next to Eve and puts her other hand on Eve's brow.

Eve You.

Celia You've cooled down a little. You were burning up. While you were asleep. Flo's left you some cakes. Christ. Cakes . . . We'll get you out of here as soon as we can.

Celia takes Eve's hand. Eve looks at her own hand.

You silly girl. Eve. You stupid, stupid . . . Sorry.

Eve I've got tiny holes, look. From the machine.

Celia No, there's no holes. You've had a fever. Could you drink some water, do you think?

Eve I used to run back from work along the marshes. Birds. Frogs. To meet you. I'd lie on my floor. In the sun.

Celia Eve. Promise me one thing.

Eve I thought you were singing that night. In the square.

Celia I should have been singing. I'm sorry.

Eve Are you going?

Celia I have to.

Eve I was very proud. To be with you.

Celia And I was proud to be with you. Terribly proud.

Nurse Time, Lady Cain.

Celia Please, we're just . . .

Eve I'm not ready to go.

Celia You're not going anywhere, darling.

Eve I haven't got my coat. Are my hands bleeding?

Celia No. No, they're not. They're not. They're not. They're not.

> *Celia kisses Eve's hands. Celia weeps. Eve strokes Celia's head.*

Eve It's alright. It's alright.

Nurse Time, miss.

> *Celia kisses Eve on the forehead and leaves. The Nurse feels Eve's pulse and records it.*

SCENE FOURTEEN

Florence's parlour. Evening. Celia sits with a drink at her side, cutting material for a banner. Florence enters with her coat and hat on. She takes her hat and gloves off.

Florence You're still here.

Celia He's late.

Florence Two hours late.

Celia Sorry, Flo. Am I in the way?

Florence No.

Celia Maybe he's changed his mind.

Florence After months of calling here like a schoolboy? He's been as nervous as a kitten. How's that going?

Celia Slow. I couldn't find your good scissors. Any news?

Florence finds her good scissors and gives them to Celia.

Florence No. But Hardie says he'd rather shoot his sons than let them become soldiers if war's declared.

Celia Schliefke called for you. Said I was to pass on the message that we're to shut down and become patriots if it happens.

Florence I saw Eve Douglas. On the Strand.

Celia Did you?

Florence We had tea.

Celia Ah. Good. How did she seem?

Florence Quite well. She's to be married. To a watch maker.

Celia Oh.

Florence Yes. In June.

Celia Bertie's adamant that he'll become a hero. Madeline's urging him to go off and return to her *couvert de gloire*. Bloody idiot. Did she seem well?

Florence She was alright. Her health's not great.

Celia pours herself another drink. There is a knock at an outside door. And a bell.

Celia William.

Florence I'll get it.

Celia What's wrong with her?

Florence She didn't go into specifics.

Florence goes to answer the door.

Celia Did she look happy?

Florence No.

Celia Was he with her?

Florence No. He was working. In Walthamstow. I've some leafleting to do. Wednesday?

Celia Yes. Thanks, Flo.

Florence takes her hat and leaves. Celia lights a cigarette. She puts a record on the phonograph. Mozart. William enters.

William Celia.

Celia nods, tries to smile.

I'm sorry I'm late. Is that everything in the hall?

Celia Yes. There's heaps of stuff, I'm afraid. Most of it's rubbish. I don't know how or why I've amassed it in three months.

William Are you alright?

Celia nods. She takes the needle off the record. William goes to her and tries to hold her, gently kiss her; it's all a bit awkward.

Celia How was your day?

William It was good. Very good. You look nice.

Celia You go on, Will. I'll be there in a moment.

William picks up her coat for her. He holds it for her to put on but she takes it from him.

William Coat.

Celia Yes. Yes, it is.

William leaves. Celia puts on her coat. She buttons it up and reaches for her hat. She is about to put it on, checking herself in the mirror, when she breaks down. She puts the record on to muffle her crying and holds herself. She now controls herself. She wipes her face and checks herself in the mirror. William walks in.

William Are you ready?

Celia Yes.

William looks at her, sees she has been crying and kisses her cheek. He passes her his handkerchief. Celia sits down. She drinks her wine. William sits next to her. He takes her hand.

William Your hand's like ice.

William covers her hand with both of his. Then breathes on it to make it warmer.

Celia Do you remember when we stayed at Yuri's dacha? We ran away from the other children playing in the evening. Into the woods. And we saw the wolf? And we watched it. And he started to walk towards us? And we both stood absolutely still. The only thing moving was our breath. And then very slowly you took my hand. Do you remember? Do you?

They sit for a few moments in silence.

William You're not coming home.

Pause. William stands and walks away from Celia. He pours himself a brandy.

Celia I thought I was. I really did.

William What made you change your mind? When did you decide this?

Celia I don't know.

William Where will you go?

Celia That wolf. It was so beautiful, Will. It broke my heart it was so beautiful.

William downs his drink and leaves. The outside door slams. Celia lights another cigarette. She smokes, reaches for her hat, puts it on. She checks herself in the mirror and leaves.

Large images of various Suffragettes come onto a screen, some together, some alone: prison images, their hair down, defiant, timeless.

Blackout.

THE PAINTER

The Painter was first performed at the Arcola Theatre, London, on 12 January 2011. The cast, in order of appearance, was as follows:

William Turner Jim Bywater
Turner Toby Jones
Sarah Danby Niamh Cusack
Jenny Cole Denise Gough
Mary Marshall Turner Amanda Boxer
Hereford / Man Ian Midlane

Director Mehmet Ergen
Set and Costumes Ben Stones
Lighting Emma Chapman
Music and Sound Adrienne Quartly
Fight Director Chris Jenkins

Characters

Turner
thirties

William Turner
his father, sixties

Mary Marshall Turner
his mother, fifties

Jenny Cole
twenties

Sarah Danby
forties

Hereford
twenties

Man in Pub

The action takes place in Turner's studio
and around London from 1799 onwards.
It covers decades, but no attempt should
be made to 'age' Turner.

SCENE ONE

The studio. 1799. William Turner varnishes a medium-sized canvas of which we can only see the back. Turner walks in from the rain. He is a touch drunk. William nods. Turner comes and looks at the canvas that William has varnished. Turner nods. Then warms himself by the wood stove.

William What did they say?

Turner says nothing. William finishes the varnishing and puts a brush in turpentine.

Did they like it? Will they take it?

Turner nods. He looks at some sketches.

You been drinking? With that lot?

Turner does not reply.

Or by yourself?

Turner By myself.

William Town was mad again. The protests. Smashing up the machines. They were climbing up and over them with their hammers. Bonfires. It was almost a riot. I'll put your supper on.

William exits. There is a large canvas on the floor. Turner walks over and looks at it.

Turner I could paint better than them with both hands tied behind my back. I could paint better than them with my tongue.

307

*He feeds various papers into the wood stove and the
light changes. Purcell's 'Dido's Lament' sounds, but
slightly distorted. He pours himself a rum. Downs it
in one. Stares at the fire. He gets on the floor and
looks at the painting close up.*

SCENE TWO

*Sarah Danby's parlour. Sarah sews. She is heavily
pregnant. Turner moves a chaise longue for her. He sets
it down.*

Sarah Thank you. That's perfect.

Turner Anything else?

Sarah No . . . I spoke to your mother yesterday. She told
me you got your Fellowship. That's wonderful. You
didn't say.

Turner Where are the girls?

Sarah They're in bed. Awake. They were outrageous
today. Screaming at each other. In the park.

Turner They miss John.

Sarah I keep thinking he'll walk through the door. Lu
talks about him. The others don't. But they know
something's happened. Mo's convinced that I might die
too. She won't let me out of her sight. She'll be out there
on the stairs in a minute. Sitting and watching me. My
sister wants us to move in with her.

Turner I thought you didn't get on.

Sarah It would be good for the girls. The countryside.
Did you never want to move out?

Turner No.

Sarah Have you found somewhere? For the gallery?

Turner Harley Street.

Sarah She's kicking. Come here, William. Feel.

Turner hesitates.

Does it scare you? . . . You might have to paint a woman with child one day.

Sarah places his hand on her stomach. He keeps it there reluctantly. And now takes it away.

Wasn't so bad, was it?

Sarah goes back to her sewing.

Your bag's in the kitchen. You always leave something behind. You should get yourself a young woman.

Turner Is there a shop for that, is there?

Sarah Will you celebrate the New Year?

Turner I saw an old man mudlarking yesterday. That'd be a nice way to see it in.

Sarah Really though? Suppose you could go anywhere? Where would you be?

Turner Rome. Paris. Amsterdam.

Sarah But if it wasn't about painting . . .? If it was just about enjoying yourself?

Turner is slightly confused.

Just any place. No galleries.

Turner . . . Maybe Archangel . . . in the snow. You?

Sarah I'd be with John. And the girls. Would you go with somebody?

Turner No.

Sarah Did you never have a girl, William?

Turner What?

Turner stares at her.

Sarah Thank you. For visiting.

Turner You're not in hospital.

Sarah I am. Sort of.

Turner stares at her.

What are you thinking about? . . . Right now.

Turner The fundamental behaviour of water.

Sarah looks away. Turner starts to leave.

Sarah William. Don't come round again.
Or . . . for a while.
It's the smell. The turpentine. It makes me feel sick.

Turner takes this in, starts to leave.

Your coat. And book . . .

Turner does not go back for them.

Goodnight, William.

Turner leaves.

SCENE THREE

Turner sits and looks through his notebooks. Noting which studies he may develop. It is late. There is a banging at his internal door. There are the sounds of a woman crying and now the throwing of objects against a wall. A bottle is smashed. William can be heard trying to calm the woman. No distinct words are heard. Turner

listens to the sounds. He stops working for a moment.
Pours himself a rum. Then he resumes.

SCENE FOUR

The next day. The studio. William stretches a canvas. He
nails it to a frame and then leans the canvas up against
several others. He takes some pigment and grinds it with
a pestle and mortar. He pours some oil into a cup. He
adds the oil to the pigment gradually. He packs a little
pipe with tobacco. Turner enters with a cup of tea,
practising Dutch.

Turner 'Heb je mijn baggage gezien?' [Phonetically, 'Hep
yee mine bahhaze heezine?']

William looks at him.

Dutch. 'Have you seen my baggage?'

Turner sees a fresh calling card on a table.

Who's this?

William A friend of Weston's. Asked about a portrait.

Turner Face painting?

William I told him that wasn't your line.

Turner puts down his tea. He studies a drawing that
is on a wooden board with a handle on it. He plunges
it into a pail of water next to him. He applies some
watercolour paint to certain areas of the picture. Now
a different wash on a few other areas. And a third
colour. He puts this board down to dry next to two
others. He takes a second drawing on a board. He
adjusts a detail or two with a pencil then plunges that
one into the pail of water and colours it with three
washes as he did the last one.

Ready for tomorrow are you?

Turner We'll leave here at one.

William You'll be an hour early. Weston's three-by-four is finished. He wants you to go for supper. See it hung up.

Turner No.

William It'll save on your mutton.

Turner Eight drawings we'll take.

William Give me a list and I'll find them.

Turner Nine just in case I got the timings wrong.

William I called on Dr Monro. Told him how things have been. He said it's only going to get worse. He described some of the treatments. They use water . . .

Turner keeps adding details. William moves towards the kitchen.

I'll put the supper on.

Turner I'm going out.

William Town'll be mad. Celebrating.

Turner Take some money. Get yourself a drink.

William No. I'll tidy up. And pack the pictures for tomorrow.

Turner puts his brush down and gathers his jacket and leaves. William starts to varnish a canvas. He lights some candles as the light fades. Varnishes some more. Then snuffs the candles and leaves the room. Dawn breaks.

SCENE FIVE

*The studio. Dawn. Turner walks in. It is dark. He holds
a candle. He is quite drunk but very controlled with it.
Jenny walks in behind him. She is a touch drunk too but
can handle herself. A woodstove glows.*

Turner You know who the woman really was?

Jenny No. You've lost me.

Turner She's his mother. Venus. Naked. Turned back
into her goddess self.

Jenny Someone kept your fire going for you. That's nice.

Turner She's toying with him. Torturing him like a cat
would a bird.

Jenny Got a dram? Of gin or something? Where can I
pee?

Turner Over there.

Jenny Ta.

> *Jenny walks behind a screen and pees while Turner
> pours some rum out from a bottle. He recites to
> Jenny.*

Turner
'For Tyrian virgins bows and quivers bear
And purple buskins o'er their ankles wear.'

> *Jenny reappears and comes to collect her drink.*

Jenny Poetry. Lovely. What next, then?

> *Jenny shivers a bit and comes to Turner and puts his
> arms on hers to warm her.*

We'll go upstairs, will we?

Turner is awkward with this.

Turner I hope so.

Jenny You don't have to hope, do you? . . . You just moved in?

Turner reaches for his bottle and glasses.

Turner No.

Jenny Can I light some more candles?

She lights the candles.

They said you were famous in the pub?

Turner No.

Turner pours out two rums and drinks one.

Jenny Is this house yours?

Turner Yes.

Jenny All of it?

Turner Yes.

Jenny I might start painting if that's what you get for it.

Turner It's not all you get.

Turner pours himself another rum.

Jenny What else?

Turner Abuse. Ignorance. Clowns telling you what your work is about.

Turner gives Jenny a rum.

Look at these.

Turner picks up some bottles of pigment.

Fugitives. No one's using them. Too scared they'll fade.

Jenny So why have you got them?

Turner I'll use them. The others won't. They'll wait.
How could you not, though? Look at them . . .

*Turner looks at the colours. Jenny looks at his
paintings.*

Jenny How come you asked me back? I thought your
models gave it out for free ?

Turner I paint trees.

Jenny laughs.

Jenny I bet some of the girls would still come over.

Turner They do. They line up. All round the building.
Every morning. Only Fridays they have a day off.

Jenny Really, though? Will girls do it with you just
because you're you?

Turner I tell you, Jane –

Jenny Jenny.

Turner I tell you, Jenny, I open my window at dawn. I
look out. Just to see what's the weather like . . . I look
up at the sky and then I look down . . . and they're all
there. Staring up at me. Hopeful. Some wear their best
clothes and others they just stand there naked, even in
the winter. It's . . . heartbreaking.

Turner pours himself another rum.

Four days after I was born there were three suns in the
sky. It was a phenomenon. What do you think that
means?

Jenny Fuck knows.

Turner I've got a good feeling about this year. Good
momentum.

Jenny They're full of promises. Abolish this. Reform that. But they never do. What about the dead? No fishing them back from the sea, is there?

Turner What? Who?

Jenny Those blacks . . . The captain threw all the sick ones overboard. In the middle of the ocean. And there were sharks everywhere. Fuck it. Let's go upstairs.

Turner says and does nothing.

I've had a lot of artists. Painters are the quietest.

Turner Really?

Jenny It's nice. Writers . . . that's a bit more like you're on the farm.

She rolls a cigarette and lights it. Turner enjoys watching her. She offers him a puff but he declines it.

I went round to model for a sculptor once. He was there in his dressing gown. Asked to see me naked. Then he started touching me all over. Slowly. He's stood behind me at one point cupping my buttocks one in each hand as if they were a fire. 'Cold?' I said. 'It is June.'

Turner What did he say?

Jenny 'I have to acquaint myself with your body in the first case. See if it'll respond. It's a very personal art.' He's breathing very hard. So I fuck off. Shall we . . .? I need to get back in a bit. To my boy.

Turner How old is he?

Turner sits down by the woodstove. He opens the woodstove and throws a stick in. It blazes up. He takes some pages from a book and puts them in the fire. They make a different light. He watches them. Turner lies down on a cushion on the floor and keeps looking at the flames. Jenny sits near him.

Jenny Four.

Turner Why did you call him Noah?

Jenny I was in Dorset and my waters broke. On the beach. They shifted me to the boarding house. I wish I'd just laid down on the pebbles for a few hours and pushed. After he was born it rained. For days. Weeks. So I called him Noah. For the sea.

Turner looks at her face properly for the first time.

What?

Turner just keeps looking.

Upstairs.
It's extra for talking.

Turner How much?

Jenny I'm joking. You're new to this, aren't you?
I could take my clothes off. You could draw me.

Turner shakes his head.

What do you like to paint best?

Turner Chaos.

Jenny Why? . . . How do you paint chaos?

Turner looks at her, smiles, shrugs his shoulders.

Do you know any of the fashionables? Have you painted them?

Turner They just want to know if a painting's hot. Whether it'll gain. They've got one or two facts. And they string them out like they were classicists.

Jenny We should do what the French did.

Turner Some of them are real. I made a couple of friends.

Jenny Fuck 'em. Even the friends. If they were friends they'd give you their castle. So you wouldn't have to ask anyone for anything.

Turner I don't ask. They ask me. They come to me.

Turner raises his hand and stays with it in the air, defiant, pissed. Jenny takes his hand down. She puts his hand on her breast. He takes it away. He gets up and walks round.
    Jenny gets up and pours herself another drink. She approaches Turner and holds him. The door opens. William looks around the door.

William . . . It's all done. Drying now.

William leaves. Jenny waits for perhaps an explanation.

Turner I think we'd best not.

Jenny You're not getting your money back.

Turner Here's something for your boy.

Turner picks up a small piece of paper with sketches on it.

Jenny It's a dragon.

Turner Does he like the water? Your lad?

Jenny Loves it. Can't keep him away from the boats and the river.
    Come and find me. I'm always in The Flag. And if I'm not, just wait a bit. I'm never out and about for long. Night.

Jenny gives Turner a kiss on the cheek and takes the picture. Turner sits and looks at a few pictures around him. William opens the door.

William Shall I lock up?

Turner Yes.

William She was . . . exotic. Goodnight.

Turner What's happening upstairs?

William She's asleep.

William leaves. Turner pours himself another rum and downs it in one. He sits back and really looks at one of the canvases. We do not see it. We just see his face. Taking it in, expressionless but intent. Studying.

SCENE SIX

The Academy. Turner stands at a lectern. William is behind him with a bundle of drawings in a portfolio. Turner addresses his students. He is terribly nervous and hungover, but trying to contain it. He has notes to read but decides to start informally. Extempore.

Turner Gentlemen I see some . . .

He looks around the invisible table, gathers himself. A pause.

New faces . . . Well, do any of you . . . Roman history . . . Is that window . . . ? Can you close it?

Pause.

There is no doubt, at least I hope not, that you are acquainted . . . not unacquainted . . . with . . .

Pause. Turner picks up a card with notes written on it.

Perspective. Gentlemen.

He reads.

'For the further advancement of the profession . . .
Looking forward with the hope that ultimately the joint
endeavours of concording abilities will . . .'

*He abandons the notes. And leans around and with
William's aid finds a picture. He holds it up. It is of
three glass balls.*

Three glass globes. With their varying reflections.

*Turner leans round again and spends some time with
William finding a different picture.*

So. Another picture. A topographical view. Topography
has reached its height in this country. There is a finite
height for it to reach unfortunately.

*Turner leans around and finds a study of a country
view.*

Copying will help you with the language of perspective.
But not with true interpretation. You will find no better
teachers than your own eyes, if you use them correctly,
to see things as they are. Excuse me. I shall resume
presently.

Turner walks away.

SCENE SEVEN

*The studio. The same evening. Turner sits across from
his mother. She stares at the floor. Then looks around.*

Mary How was it? With the men?
    They were coming to buy.

Turner It went well.

Mary You're surprised.
    You didn't think I'd remember . . .

320

Turner does not reply.

When I'm clear I'm lucid.

Turner Absolutely. I know that.

Mary Don't.

Turner What?

Mary Your tone. It was patronising . . . How's your copying?

Turner I haven't copied for years.

Mary See. We're talking, aren't we?

Turner nods.

Nobody's rattling pans or spitting. There are some important collectors coming round. Next week.

Turner That's right. Fawkes recommended them.

Mary He recommended you, not them. You're the one he's helping.

Turner It works both ways.

Mary I know. About your decision.

Turner is wrong-footed.

Turner Which decision?

Mary I thought I was somewhere else just now. So you've decided.

Turner Decided what?

Mary Why do you want me put away?

Turner I don't, Ma.

Mary Why do you insist on calling me that? I'd prefer it if you didn't. Monro's your patron. You asked him his opinion about me. How could you do that?

Turner He's a doctor.

Mary You've betrayed me . . . You've consulted Monro. And told him I was mad.

Turner I didn't say that.

Mary Are you sending me to Bedlam?

Turner No. Monro said St Luke's would be good for you.

Mary Pa visited the lunatics. He paid his entrance fee. He liked the spectacle of it. He said it stank. And a woman gave birth on a floor covered in shit. Is that where you want me?

Turner St Luke's is clean. Reputable.

Mary Like you? You're selling me to the Indians. Filial. You never felt that did you? I never wanted your father. Or you.

Turner I'll make you some tea.

Mary You sound like one of your fashionables. All they can feel is fear. And it's rubbing off on you. They smother their embarrassment and terror with all their gabble.

Turner You keep cutting yourself.

Mary I'm making marks not cutting. It's protection. It moves the pain away from my head. Shame you feel. So did he. You've had advantages, though.

Turner Advantages?

Mary I never hurt you when you were a child. I never would have hurt you. I didn't, did I? They say you're worth a fortune. All because you can copy things.

Turner does not reply, despondent. Mary reaches out her hand to him. Turner moves slowly to take her hand. As he touches hers Mary takes her hand slowly from his. Shakes her head.

You remind me of a dog. At people's feet. Waiting to be liked. Stroked.

Turner moves away from her.

I thought I was at the farm. Your heart's a hole, Billy. At least I can feel. Even if it's only pain. You can love some waterfall but you can't feel anything for your own mother. If they were letting my blood you'd only want to get in the room to paint it.

Turner nods, sighs, Mary stares away from him.

Take my hand. I'm sorry. Love's all that matters. To love and to forgive. It's not about who's right. But who's in the most pain.

Turner takes his mother's hand.

When are they coming for me?

Turner Monro needs to visit.

Mary You're selling me like a black. For being different. You're nothing to me now, Billy. Don't cry. Don't be sad. Because there is nothing. Between us. Get your pencils. Go and do your copying.

Turner does not move.

SCENE EIGHT

A pub. William sits and drinks, across from a Man, who is drinking too. William has had a few beers.

William They killed it. With the taxes.

Man Your shop?

William Wigs. A full one, that's really something. You've got your needle. That's like a fishing hook. You take a couple of strands of hair. And knot them in. And you just keep doing that . . . maybe thirty to forty thousand times. Working both hands all the time to keep the tension.

William drinks.

I took up cutting instead. It paid the rent. But in the end it's a lot of dead hair round your feet. Whereas a wig, it's . . . it's . . .

William raises his glass to the Man who toasts with him.

Man A wig.
Make money with it, did you?

William It was a living. There's a new bloke in the market. Swallowing snakes he is. I asked him if it hurt. 'No,' he says. 'You just pinch their tail and they'll hop in there. They can get through tiny holes. Smaller than you think.' It makes itself into a ball. Down his throat. Then he pulls it back. That's when it hurts. He used to gag. But now he's got used to it.

Man Did he have much of a crowd?

William No.

Man Did you give him anything?

William I gave him a bit. Sleeping rough, he is. Him and his snakes. My wife was the most beautiful woman you ever saw in your life. Touch something she would and people would want to give it to her whatever it was. Like she was some Hindu goddess. With a shrine. She'd brush past a piece of furniture with her hand. Pale. Long fingers. And whoever's it was, they'd say, 'Take it. You like it? Take it.'

Man How does he live with that? A snake? In and out of his throat.

William Same again?

William gets up from the table.

SCENE NINE

The studio. Turner studies a book of lithographs. A knock on the door.

Turner Come in.

Jenny walks in.

Jenny Sorry I'm late. I've been running around . . . These pictures of me. Who are they for?

Turner No one.

Jenny Can I have a drink?

Turner It's there.

Jenny pours herself a gin.

Jenny Will you have one?

Turner No.

Jenny starts to prepare the space for her pose, cushions, a sheet.

Jenny Why don't you use corpses?

Turner No. There's no breath. No movement.

Jenny You paint trees. They don't move.

Turner Course they do. They're always moving.

Jenny Are you doing men like this too?

Turner No.

Jenny Not interested?

Turner Too ugly.

Jenny laughs and pours another gin from the bottle.

Jenny Noah did some drawings for you with that paper you sent. Fuck, I meant to bring them.

Turner prepares his paper to sketch again. Jenny downs her gin in one.

We waved goodbye to you. From the cliff. But you didn't see. You were down on the dock. Staring at the sun. For ages. Doesn't that hurt your eyes?

Turner Same as you staring at a candle.

Jenny He had a great day. Thanks. He's still talking about it. How come you paint the sea such a lot?

Turner It's the light. And what's underneath. Terrifying. Can you swim?

Jenny No. I don't like it.

Turner I'll take you and Noah down to Margate. Teach you how.

Jenny Will you show us where you lived?

Turner Nothing to see.

Jenny Why did they send you there?

Turner My mother was ill. Shall we make a start?

Jenny I can't imagine you swimming.

Turner It's the only time I don't feel short. If I wasn't a painter I'd be a sailor.

Jenny smiles.

Jenny Seriously? If I wasn't a prozzy I'd be . . . Happy. I should stop really. I did try other stuff. Pins. Fuck pins. Then slop work. Shirts. Buttons.

Turner Don't move your top half for a minute.

Jenny I could get by on it. But not when it became the two of us . . . I did look for other work. But there was nothing. It was winter. Noah's legs one night – they went blue. I rubbed brandy all over him. I was terrified. I ran down to the workhouse with him in my arms. I'd always sworn I'd never go there . . . and the fuckers, they wouldn't let me in. Not without an order. So I did it.

Turner We'll do an hour. Three different poses.

Jenny pours herself one more drink.

Jenny The first time was horrible. I was terrified. I pretended I'd been at it for ages. Stupid. I could have made more if I'd said I was new. You know what they do to the young girls? To make the men think it's her first time . . . ?

They put leeches up her. So when he's inside her he doesn't notice she's ripped already. But he gets a sting and he thinks that's it. If the girl's funny about leeches they'll –

Turner Don't . . .

Jenny They'll put a few tiny bits of broken glass up her. Just enough to make a bit of blood flow . . . Me, I don't mind what happens. I'm old. But with them. It's not right. They're very young.

Turner pours himself a rum and downs it in one.

I was picked up for it just the once. A constable. He took me outside and questioned me.

Turner What happened?

Jenny He asked me how long I'd been whoring. He was quite excited. And drunk. I made myself cry. 'I'm so sorry,' I said. 'You're right. I did give in to his copious solicitations.' I thought he'd fine me. Or ask for one. That's what most of them do. I was hoping it'd be against the wall because he was huge. He'd be pretty heavy on top. But he just went a bit red and let me go. Mags, though. Last year. She was shipped off to Sydney. Australia.

Turner For whoring?

Jenny And running a disorderly house. It wasn't so much that. Someone had lost their watch. They don't give a fuck about girls and broken glass but as soon as it's about property they're down on you like anything. Probably she did steal it. But still. Fuck. For a pocket watch. 'A Noted Virago', the papers called her.
She was tough. Fierce. If your man hit her she hit him back. Have you been in fights?

Turner No. Not with a man. Lower body now.

Jenny lies back down on the floor and now pulls her skirts up and her legs further apart so that Turner can see her nakedness although we do not. He stands and prepares to sketch.

Jenny Like that?

Turner and Jenny take a few moments to get over the strangeness of the situation.

Are you comfortable up there, are you? Mr Turner?

Turner 'He who would search for pearls must dive below.'

Jenny Will you take yourself off upstairs after I've gone?

Turner cannot reply.

Turner Hermaphrodites.

Jenny What?

Turner Half man, half woman. The Greeks believed we were all both sexes in one body originally. Then we were cut in two. And the rest of our lives is a search for that lost half.

Jenny So half of me is a man somewhere? And half of you is a woman?

Turner If she looks like me I don't want to find her.

Jenny smiles. Turner settles down now and sketches. A knock on the door. Turner does not leave his drawing and shouts through.

No!

Another knock.

Not in. Working.

The door opens and Sarah walks in, but Turner does not look round to see her.

Leave it outside the door.

Sarah I'm sorry. But I was troubled.

Turner looks around.

Turner Sarah . . .

Sarah You're working. I'll only be a moment.

Sarah walks towards Turner.

I'm sorry. About the other evening.

Turner It's not the best time.

Sarah I only want a minute.

Sarah sees Jenny now. Tries not to be too wrong-footed.

Oh. I see. I'm . . . interrupting. You should have said. You're . . . involved.

Jenny sits up, pulls her clothes around her.

Turner It's –

Sarah I'm sorry. Excuse me. I didn't realise you –

Turner It's anatomy.

Sarah Yes.

Turner The female form.

Sarah Yes. I see that.

She leaves. Turner puts down his drawing board. Breathes. Jenny stands up.

Jenny Who was that?

Turner A neighbour.

Jenny Married?

Turner Her husband just died.

Jenny Everyone loves widows.
She likes you.
She's nice looking. Tight, though. Her face. She wants you.

Jenny sees something of the sketch.

Strange looking, aren't we? Does it come out exactly as you want it to?

Turner No. That's the work of it.

Jenny When you're looking at things, do you just see them as pictures?

Turner I'm waiting a lot of the time. Sifting stuff.

Jenny What would you do? If you couldn't see?

Turner I'd kill myself, no question. You?

Jenny I couldn't. Not with Noah.

Jenny closes her eyes. She feels her own face a little. Then Turner's arm and his face. Then she opens them.

Billy, I saw a man. On London Bridge. Did I tell you? No. It was Thursday. He was shouting. Pissed. Swaying. He had no shoes. He'd taken his shirt off and he was saying he'd jump. He was being so loud about it and I thought he was just looking for attention. I walked past on the other side. And I swear he seemed to be staring at me. He went quiet then. And he just stepped off . . . as though there was a platform. In the air. I felt sick, Billy. Like I'd be sick.

Jenny becomes melancholic. She weeps.

Sorry, Billy. It's just the gin. But it is the fucking loneliest city in the world, London. Isn't it?

Jenny lies down again. She starts to really cry now, weepy with the drink. Turner keeps drawing her.

SCENE TEN

The Academy. Turner lectures to his students. He is still nervous, but has abandoned the formal cards. He has a large notebook he can refer to.

Turner If you'd like to sit if you're going to stay . . .
And could you close that door . . . ?

The sublime. A dark event. A maelstrom. It can have
its own beauty. The captain of a slave ship.
Collingwood. He is told that he will receive insurance
for any blacks who are lost at sea. But not for those who
are dead on arrival. He does not want to lose money, so
he inspects the hulls. He gathers up those slaves who are
sick and might not last the journey. He marches them up
on to the deck. In the middle of the night. The sea is
black. And shark infested. He has his men remove the
slaves' shackles. And then throws them overboard. They
scream. Struggle. Cry out for some minutes. And then
they are simply the sound of the sea. He suspects his
crime is hidden in the vastness of that ocean. Under cover
of night. A sailor recounts it. It is up to us to paint it.
Record it. Put that man on trial for the rest of history.
Forget about dogs. Face-painting. Flowers. There is
sometimes a duty. To record. And to paint such violence
but with a beauty – that would be something. We'll
resume. Presently.

Turner leaves.

SCENE ELEVEN

*The studio. William hauls in long herring nets. Two
stepladders are at either side of the walls. Turner comes
in and together they hang the nets high up and flat near
the ceiling. Then Turner lays tissue paper on the nets. He
steps down and looks at a picture on the wall. William
observes Turner and the picture. Turner looks up at the
light as it diffuses through the tissue. Bright sunshine
streams through.*

William How is it?

332

Turner nods. Watches the painting again. He climbs up a ladder to adjust the tissue. Comes down. Looks. Nods.

Yes?

Turner It'll have to be bigger. Everything'll be scaled up by maybe twenty.

William But it works in principle?

Turner The light's good. It's diffusing.

William More nets, then.

A door closes in the next room to theirs.

Turner We'll get them sewn together into one, else there'll be seams. Lines in the light. It's got to be perfect. And we'll paint the walls red.

William Red?

Turner Carmine. And vermilion.

William Red.

Turner They laugh at me.

William Who?

Turner At the Academy. They think I'm out of my depth. The wrong class.

William No.

Turner They do. But no matter.

William I looked at their work.

Turner What did you think?

William Nice lines. No ideas.

Turner Who's next door?

William looks through a spy-hole in the wall.

William It's the widow.

Turner looks through the spy-hole.

Turner Can you tell her I'm not in?

William No.

Turner does not answer. Turner starts to line some wood up for stretchers. William leaves. Turner starts to make a frame to stretch a canvas on. He measures the wood.

A gentle knock. Sarah walks in and watches him. She is behind him. She starts to walk towards him and he hears her and looks at her. He is on his knees. He gets up.

Turner Hello.

Turner puts his tools down.

How are you?

Sarah I've brought your books.

Turner and Sarah look at each other. He measures up another piece of wood.

Turner I'm sorry. If you felt . . . awkward . . . the other night.

Sarah I blushed. That was all.

Pause. Turner shows Sarah a red pigment.

Turner What do you think of this? For the gallery?

Sarah It looks like Napoleon's bedroom.

Turner He's got a David he hangs in his bathroom. Philistine. He was teased. About his accent. He couldn't spell.

Sarah Do you admire him?

Turner He's a butcher. But his numbers are impressive.

Turner looks at the books that Sarah has returned, awkward.

Sarah It wasn't that girl's nudity that made me blush. I've seen enough of that backstage. It was her being so near to you.

Turner She's a model.

Sarah And a prostitute.

Turner She tried other stuff.

Sarah You defend her.

Turner What?

Sarah We keep doing this. Missing each other's mark.

Turner takes a knife and starts to cut some wood.

Be careful . . . of your hands.

Sarah picks up a sketch.

You work too hard.

Turner Rubens produced three thousand paintings. Harley Street's got to be the biggest. The best.

Sarah Why?

Turner It's going to be epic. We can fit a hundred people in there.

Sarah But you produce work for yourself, don't you?

Turner It's by me. Not for me. You didn't act for yourself, did you?

Sarah It's sad that money ever has to come into the equation.

Turner Is it? Velazquez always wanted a knighthood. He petitioned everyone. Even the Pope. He had to write a letter apologising for ever having asked for money for his work. Because a gentleman would never do that. They kept refusing him.

Sarah Did he ever get it?

Turner A year before he died . . . People think that the act of putting paint on canvas, that should be enough of a reward. But it's a dance . . . Velazquez! Writing a letter. Of apology.

Sarah Would you like a knighthood? Would that settle you?

Turner I'm not ill.

Sarah But you chase.

Turner No. I work. I record. That's what I do.

Sarah I've offended you.

Turner They'd never have me in their stable anyway. Constable, maybe. Not me. A rough at court? No. 'Mr Turner, alas, feels the perpetual need to be extraordinary.' Why would you want to be anything else?

Sarah You shouldn't read reviews.

Turner A friend quoted it to me . . . You're extraordinary. When you act.

Sarah I won't be able to go back to it. I'm sorry – that our friendship has gone awry.

Turner Has it?

Sarah Who's the best out of Rubens and Velazquez?

Turner Velazquez almost puts your eyes out he's so good. And Titian. And Claude. Fuseli. France I need to

get to. Italy. What's here is mostly useless. English
painting is dead. It's dealers making fortunes out of
sentimental dross. Dogs. Cherubs.

*Sarah sees a circle wheel of colour on paper with
tones from dark to light on it.*

Sarah What's this?

Turner It's the tonal scale. From Rooker. Watercolours
they're transparent. So you work from light to dark. I'll
work on maybe four at the same time. Do the first tone
on all of them. Then the second.

Sarah looks at an open sketchbook.

Sarah And these are of where?

Turner Yorkshire. It rained so much I was webfoot.

Sarah Webfoot?

Turner I was. Like a drake.

Sarah You're different in here.
You're freer.

*Turner looks at Sarah. She smiles. They look at each
other properly for the first time.*

William.

Turner Yes?

Sarah Why were you angry when I talked about your
love life?

Turner I haven't got a love life. So you couldn't be
talking about it. Could you? I wasn't. Angry.

Turner kneels down to sort the stretchers.

Sarah Why haven't you got one?

Turner If I went out somewhere I'd want to take my sketchbook with me. And girls don't like the smell of paint.

Sarah I didn't mean it when I said that.

Sarah stands into him so that her skirt is next to him. He ignores the touch of the material. Sarah goes to her knees and kisses him. Turner kisses her strongly. Then stops.

Turner Sorry.

Sarah Why? Lie next to me.

Turner I've thought about that.

Sarah Have you?

Turner A lot.

Sarah You should have said.

Turner I didn't imagine . . .

Sarah That I wanted that? I do.

Sarah kisses Turner. They become very passionate. Turner breaks away.

Turner Sorry.

Sarah You need to think less.
  Let your guard down. Trip up. Fall down. Between my legs.

Turner Am I allowed to think about that?

Sarah You are.

He kisses her again. Then stops. Takes her face in his hands and looks at her intently.

Turner Come upstairs. Please.

Sarah Don't say please.

Turner Come upstairs.

Sarah Yes.

Turner Thank you.

Turner realises he should not have thanked Sarah. He walks towards the door in front of her, then opens it for her.

SCENE TWELVE

Six months later. The studio. Mary sits. William stands, waiting for Turner. There is a travelling bag next to her.

Mary He carries on with her but he won't marry?

William I'll take your bag for you.

Mary Leave it. Months he's been going to hers after dark. Like some sort of animal.

Turner enters with Sarah.

Turner Monro's outside. He's waiting for the coach.

Mary The baby's not yours. The widow's child.

Sarah Mary . . . how are you?

Mary Your musician. His hands changed. They became like hooks.

Sarah They did. He died.

Mary He couldn't play any more. But they're not locking him up. Another child you have.

Sarah Yes. John's baby.

Mary But you two . . . carry on.

Turner does not reply.

Sarah William has helped me. A great deal.

Mary He's not helped me. You've been kind, Sarah. These two weren't. At least your John died at home. With windows. I have been through such violence. In my head.

Sarah Perhaps . . . at the hospital . . .

Turner Monro says the doctors there are the best.

Mary He says a lot. I shan't need my clothes.

Sarah You will. Of course you will.

Mary No I won't. They're worried that I might kill myself in my bedroom. But I think it would be kinder to let me hang from a rafter here than fester there.

Sarah The treatments . . . they might alleviate the pain. And then you can come home.

Mary They won't have me here, Sarah. They just won't.

She takes some clothes out of her bag.

Sarah Mary . . .

Mary I shan't need them.

Sarah Let's put them back. They'll hang them up for you there.

Mary I'm not a child. I know what they do. They keep you naked there. I want nothing from here. I shall have to stop talking soon. We'll all stop talking. And then it will be time.

William I'll see if the coach is here.

Mary Don't. They'll come in. Am I keeping you from something? More important?

Turner Ma . . . don't.

Mary Don't what? What am I not to do now? Sarah, don't trust these men. They're cold. And they'll try to kill you. They will.

Mary hangs her underwear over Turner's canvases.

So. I take my leave of you. Come and draw me in there. Dead. You wouldn't save me if I was drowning, would you, Billy? Your money. It's nothing. It's filthy. You're all on the inside. Since it happened to me they're all trying to get in. I need someone from the outside. To hear me. Someone who's not biased. Prejudice is a terrible thing. They all want to violate me. As if I was a girl again. The men from the market came here this morning. Lining up for me. Shouting. They want to lock me in a shed somewhere and use me there. Like a heifer. And you don't stop them, Billy. You say 'Ma this' and 'Ma that' but you just stand there and do nothing.

A man waits outside for Mary. William gathers her clothes in her case. Turner exits. Sarah follows him. William guides Mary gently by the shoulders.

Who are you? Running around after him. Like a lackey. I hate you.

William nods.

I hate you.
I hate you. Help me.

William holds Mary. They hold each other. Then William attempts to lead her out of the room. Turner appears at the door with Sarah.

I need to say goodbye. To Billy. Alone.

Turner walks in. William walks out. Sarah starts to walk away.

341

Turner Sarah. Stay.

Sarah Your mother wants to say goodbye to you.

Turner Please. Stay.

Sarah stands near the door, half there, half not. Mary puts her hand out to Turner. He walks to her and takes it.

Mary When you were a boy I would take you down to the docks. And sometimes when the ebb tide was at flood the river was so high that the boats would shoot over London Bridge – do you remember that?

Turner nods.

I bought you a paint box. For Christmas. In a wooden case. You were ten. I put it by your bed. In the dark. And you woke. And your hands shook when you were opening it. I had to help you because you were so excited.

Turner You'd drawn on the paper.

Mary I only prayed the once. Truly prayed. When your sister was dying. The Christmas after that one. Mary. She was eight. Do you remember?

Turner Yes.

Mary I knelt on the ground. I looked at her face. Fevered. In pain. And I looked at you stood by the door. Watching us all. And I prayed. I said, 'God, please, if you could just take one of my children, then take Billy. Let Mary live.' You weren't even ill but I said, 'Billy can die, God. But please let me keep my daughter.'

Turner takes his hand away from his mother.

What? She was beautiful, wasn't she? Your sister? She was an angel.

Mary walks out. Turner stands there and Sarah joins him now. And they hold each other.

SCENE THIRTEEN

The Academy. Turner lectures to his students.

For composition. Respect your paper. Keep your corners quiet. Centre your interest.

Mechanical rules. You may be a genius, but you must first learn your craft. Rules are not fetters. They only limit those with no talent. For those who are strong they are a defence. For those who are weak and confused rules are indeed shackles.

You, sir, you seem to be enjoying a conversation in the back there . . . You drew a dog last week, didn't you? A dog with an open mouth. And legs that would not support a chicken. We will resume. Imminently.

SCENE FOURTEEN

The studio. Jenny wanders round, looking at drawings. She goes to a mirror and looks at her face. She finds some water in a basin and cleans off some of her rouge. Turner walks in.

Turner Jenny. You're early.

Jenny On time. That's a first, isn't it?

Turner You look different.

Jenny How's your week been? Mine's been mayhem. Thank God for Kent. If we didn't go there I'd go mad, I really would. Noah sent you some pictures.

Jenny gives a roll of a few pictures to Turner. He does not undo them.

Turner Thank him for me.

Jenny You'll see him. At the weekend. Are you not going to have a look? He did a crocodile. And a pirate ship. He used that triangle thing you showed him . . . What is it?

Turner Why?

Jenny You always look at them.

Turner I will. Later.

Jenny Is something wrong?

Turner No. Nothing's wrong. I . . .

Jenny Has something happened?

Turner No. Yes.

Jenny Are you chucking me out?

Turner What?

Jenny She's told you to clear out your studio. Have a good clean. Get rid of all the filth.

Turner No . . .

Jenny Oh. Good. What then?

Turner Yes. She has.

Jenny I thought so. I'm surprised she left it this long. She's got a point. I wouldn't want my fella staring into some other woman's cunt. No matter.

Turner I've got some money for you. Because there was no notice.

Jenny Keep it . . . Spend it on Noah. It's a shame. It was very . . . peaceful. Are we doing today's session?

Turner No.

Jenny So . . . I've an hour to do exactly what I please. I'll just put something warmer on.

Jenny takes some woollen garments from her bag. She stands away from Turner and takes off her shirt so that her back is to him and naked. He is aware of her.

It's nice. Being painted. You sit back and go places. Last week I closed my eyes and I kept seeing all those orchards we passed. And those rows and rows of hops. Everything slows down. I'll miss the smell. Maybe I'll take some jars. To remind me.

Jenny, dressed now, goes to Turner and shakes his hand.

Thanks. It's been great. So I'll see you on Saturday. At the station. Same time as usual.

Turner looks awkward.

Won't I?

Turner I can't.

Jenny What?

Turner She wants me to stop seeing you. Altogether.

Jenny But he's a child. He won't understand. She's a . . . We've never touched each other. Not once.

Turner Sarah asked if I was his dad.

Jenny He's four years old. What is she, a fucking halfwit?

Turner She thinks I'm lying about it.

Jenny Suspicious fucking bitch. What do you talk about with her?

Turner What?

Jenny Does she make you laugh? No.

Turner What?

Jenny You're worth more than that. Why did you agree to it?

Turner She was upset.

Jenny I'm upset. All of London's upset. Every fucking day. Doesn't mean you can take it out on some innocent stranger.

Turner I'm sorry.

Jenny No, you're not. You never do a thing that you don't want to do. Do you love her?

Turner does not answer.

Do you love anyone?

Turner Take the money.

Jenny Keep your fucking blood money. She's trained you. Some people fall in love and some simply train each other up.

Turner Nobody's trained me.

Jenny You're her dog.

Turner I'm not her fucking dog –

Jenny She's got you jumping and you don't even know that you're doing it.

Turner She needs me. She's got four daughters.

Jenny You're a coward, Billy. You only met her because she lives next fucking door. You hide in here and you're terrified of anything approaching real life. No matter. We're all as bad as each other. I'll see you, then.

Jenny goes to Turner and they hold each other and she gives him a gentle kiss on the cheek. They don't want to let each other go. Turner kisses Jenny's neck. She kisses him back. They kiss. She stops kissing him now, but stays in his arms.

Jenny I'm not . . . I don't . . . I've been drinking gin all day.

Turner You don't taste of gin.

Jenny kisses him again. Then starts to leave, upset. She walks back towards him.

Jenny I told Noah you were his dad . . . I told him you were his father, but we couldn't all be together.

Turner What? Why would you say that?

Jenny When he was ill. He said he wished you were his dad. So I told him you were. But that it was a secret. You're the only man he's known, Billy. Who's been kind to him. He talks about you. He points to men who are fishing in the distance and asks if they're you. He waves at boats. Asks if you're on them. You taught him things.

Turner Children shouldn't be lied to. He won't thank you for it. When he's older.

Jenny I don't think he'll make it that far . . . You don't see him nights. And I don't give a fuck about the truth. Who's to say you weren't his dad for a few months?

Turner I'm not . . . his dad.

Jenny What's a father anyway?

Turner It's not me.

Jenny No. Maybe not . . . but I'd say anything to make him that bit happier. You don't know. You've not had a child. I worry about him . . . And I worry about you. That you'll never let yourself fall. Truly.

Turner I should get on now. Take that money. Really.

Jenny No. You can't even let me say goodbye. You're a beautiful hypocrite, Billy. You're scared and you don't even know it. You want to try just living for a change sometime. See how it feels.

Turner I do live . . . I do. Just . . . somewhere else.

Jenny walks out.

SCENE FIFTEEN

The Academy. Turner lectures.

Nature is wild. Cruel. Never be afraid to put your brightest light next to your deepest shadow on the centre. But not in the corners. You must mark the greater from the lesser truth. Express the larger idea, not the narrow and confined. Landscapes are seen as static. Rooted. They're not. Don't be a slave to what you see. It may rain. You don't have to paint it. Look past it. Select, combine and concentrate that which is beautiful. Hannibal . . . he chose to . . . no matter. We'll resume presently.

Turner leaves.

SCENE SIXTEEN

The studio. Turner notes something down in a book. Sarah knits.

Sarah What are you writing?

Turner Nothing.

A beat.

Sarah Did you talk to . . . ?

Turner Yes.

Sarah How was she about it?

Turner Dignified.

Sarah Were you ever her . . . client?

Turner No.

Sarah Were you somebody else's?

Turner Why do you want to know?

Sarah Because I'm with you. I asked you to do something that meant a lot to me. I didn't demand it. Or dictate it.

Turner I asked you for something.

Sarah I don't want you to draw me like that.

Turner I didn't want to turn Jenny out.

Sarah You talk as though she were living with you.

Turner She was a friend. She was the closest I've ever had to a sister.

Sarah I hope that's not how your sister would have ended up.

Turner You were an actress.

Sarah That doesn't mean I was a whore. But she is. A whore. I'm not judging her. I'm stating what she is.

Turner She's got a boy to support. She's a good mother.

349

Sarah I've four daughters. It's what women do.

Turner He's a sweet boy.

Sarah You've met him?

Turner We took him down to see the ships. In Margate. He'd never seen the sea. He was fantastic. Racing the waves he was.

Sarah You don't take the girls out. With me. We live as though someone will cut our throats if we were ever to play happy families.

Turner I don't know that we're . . .

Sarah What?

Turner We started out well.

Sarah We're not a horserace . . . It's not been long. Give it time. We need to attune.

Turner Do we? Don't people simply . . . ?

Sarah No. They don't. It takes time. And practice.

Turner Training . . . Sarah . . .

Sarah Yes?
William . . .

Sarah takes his hand and puts it against her stomach. She puts his hand just above her pubis bone.

Can you feel that? How it's harder there? My stomach. It's my womb. That's us. There.

Turner You're . . . ?

Sarah Yes.
Kiss me. And keep your hand on my stomach.

They kiss.

Turner Do you love me?

Sarah You've to think less, William. Billy. Just trust. I'm here. We're here.

She kisses him.

Turner Will you leave? Or change? Towards me?

Sarah No.

Turner Never?

Sarah Never.

Turner When you acted, did it feel like lying?

Sarah No. Never.

Turner looks at Sarah's stomach. She kisses him lightly. Turner breathes, kisses her strongly.

SCENE SEVENTEEN

Six months later. Turner writes a list in his notebook. William enters, distracted. Hereford looks in at the door, visible to us but not to father and son.

Turner Take the day off if you want to.

William I don't. We're busy. There's a buyer waiting.

Turner I don't want to see anyone. Why don't these people give us some notice? It's not a fucking soup kitchen . . .

Hereford I'm here, Mr Turner. I'm sorry if I'm . . . but I have travelled. I didn't know there was a system in place.

Turner An appointment will do.

Hereford I'd like an hour if you can spare it.

Turner I can't.

Hereford I want to buy a few pieces. I'm quite serious.

Turner I'm serious too.

Hereford enters and William leaves.

Hereford Of course. Time is money.

Turner No. Time is time.

Hereford cannot reply.

You want something big or you want something small?

Hereford Monro said you had a dry sense of humour.

Hereford sees some dried-up paint brushes.

Are these pencils done for? In which case I'd buy them off you.

Turner I'm not dead . . . If you could be brief I would appreciate it.

Hereford I'm an admirer. A fanatic. It's fascinating for me. To see you in your own environment. You're the first in your department, Mr Turner, you really are.

Turner does not reply.

I own a bit of everyone. But nothing of yours yet. Weston said there was talk of Twickenham. And a floating studio?

Turner I might buy a boat.

Hereford Wonderful. Giles Hereford. Lloyds of London. I collect internationally. For my own viewing. Not for commercial use.

Turner There's a body of my work at the Academy at the moment. If you'd like to have a look. Here is anarchy. As you can see.

Hereford looks at a canvas.

Hereford These are very nice. Your arboreal forms.

Turner Trees.

Hereford Do you need more staff? I know people. It's probably a bit much for the old boy, isn't it?

Turner He starts the paintings and he finishes them.

Hereford laughs.

Hereford It's good to keep the ancient employed.

Turner You shouldn't talk of the old like that.
He's my father.

Hereford nods, awkward.

Hereford I paint. As well as collect. So I do understand. The process.

Turner What do you paint?

Hereford Anything. Everything.

Turner Then you're making a mistake before you even start. Do you sketch?

Hereford Regularly.

Turner How many times will you record a subject?

Hereford Once . . . generally.

Turner . . . What colour is your front door?

Hereford Black.

Turner Describe it to me.

Hereford It's black.

Turner Show me your hands.

Hereford takes off his gloves and shows Turner his clean hands.

You're not a painter.

Hereford Not everyone uses their fingers. Or spits on the canvas.

Turner Fuck off.

Hereford looks at Turner.

I just asked you to leave.

Hereford I heard you.

Pause.

So . . . I'll buy elsewhere.

Turner Good. Go on then. You've met your hero, now fuck off.

Hereford I'm sorry. That we couldn't talk. Properly.

Turner breathes heavily. He sits now. He puts his head between his hands. Hereford watches, fascinated. He is in no hurry to leave.

Mr Turner? Are you not well? Shall I get you something?

Turner does not move.

Some water?

William looks in through the door. He comes straight in to Turner and holds him tight.

William Billy. Billy? It's all right. Don't get yourself in a state about it.

Hereford He just seemed to . . .

William His mother. They moved her today. From hospital.

Hereford To where?

William To Bedlam.
  It's all right, Billy.

354

Hereford still watches the famous man in his emotion.

William Fuck off, will you? My son's not well. Or can't you see that?

Hereford nods, leaves.

Billy.

William gives Turner a cup of water. Turner gets up and walks to the back of the studio. He goes behind the screen and is sick into a bucket, his back to his father.

That's all right. Best get it out.

Turner comes out, wipes himself with a rag.

You need to stop today. Rest.

Turner She said how her dad had paid to watch the inmates before. Like a circus.

William They don't do that now. No paying public.

Turner They're still in there, though, aren't they? They're just invisible.

Father and son sit, not touching, trying to take in the situation.

SCENE EIGHTEEN

The studio. Sarah walks around looking at the sketches. She is heavily pregnant now. She is looking for the series that depicts Jenny. She looks at a book. A newspaper clipping falls out. Sarah picks it up. Reads it. William walks in.

William Sarah.

Sarah Hello.

William Don't see you in here often.

Sarah He's saved this. 'Mr Turner, whose genius we so much admire, has been long trifling with his fame, and playing upon the borders of extravagance as if in pursuit of his attainment. We hope, now he has reached it, he may be induced to abandon these experiments.'

William Bastards. He's at the Academy.

Sarah I know. We'll all go later, will we?

William In your condition?

Sarah Of course. I was looking. For William's anatomical sketches. Of Jenny . . . How was the visit? To Mrs Turner.

William They'd cut all her hair off. Looked like they'd used a knife. Blood and . . . all over her head. They don't bother to clean them up very much. It's not very clever.

Sarah Does she know where she is?

William She fades in and out.

Sarah What did Monro say?

William That the descent will be fast. A few weeks, he said.

Sarah William refuses to go there.

William I can't force him.

Sarah I'm sorry. What was he like? As a boy?

William He'd always be looking up. Other children they'd be looking down. To find stuff. Anything. On the streets. He'd be staring up. At the sky.

Sarah And Mary was ill even then?

William It was always there. Less evident, though.

Sarah He said she couldn't stand to be in the same room as him.

William Cruel, she was. Said things a child should never hear. Did things he never should have seen. And when little Mary died she just lost it. She'd lock herself up. Disappear. I'd take him down to see the boats. Teach him to swim. And fish. He only wanted to please her. We both did.

Sarah He should see her, don't you think? For his own peace of mind.

William He's terrified he'll end up like her. He thinks it's in him. The madness.

Sarah He doesn't want me here any more. He hasn't said it. But I can feel it. I thought that our having a child might change things.

William I should put the meat on.

Sarah I do love him, William.

William starts to study a canvas.

As much as you can love somebody who's absent.

The outside door goes. William shouts.

William Billy? You're back early? How was it?

Turner walks in from the street, carrying a portfolio.

Turner It was . . . good. Sarah.

Sarah Hello.

Turner Hello.

Turner takes a breath. Calms down. He pours himself a rum.

I wish you'd been there, Dad. You should have come. They were hysterical. Running around. No amount of light is going to repair some of those monsters they've created.

William Lots of rubbish?

Turner Most of it's woefully weak. There's a few interesting ones.

William Any trouble?

Turner No. They put me in the best space. It looks impressive.

William It'll sell then?

Turner I took it off the list. I'm not going to sell it.

William What do you mean?

Turner It's one of the family.

William You're joking me.

Turner No. We don't need the money.

William You're soft, Billy.

Turner Am I? No. No, it's a good decision

William walks out.

Sarah That's lovely. That you'll keep it.

Turner I'm tired of them all going away.

Sarah Are you looking forward to the child? Our child.

Turner I am.

Sarah Are you? You're always . . . somewhere else.

Turner No.

William walks in.

William I've put some stew on. We can eat early.

Sarah We could eat at Rule's on the way? We're celebrating, aren't we?

William and Turner share a look.

Turner You've made it now, haven't you?

William Chopped. Not cooked.

Turner Let's eat here. I can't face any more of all that today.

William How much would they have to offer to make you change your mind?

Turner No amount. I'd like to be buried in it if I'm honest.

William What?

Turner Have it as my winding sheet. In the earth.

William I'll get changed. Have a wash.

He exits.

Sarah You've money but you won't eat out.

Turner It's all the . . . service. And people doing things for you. And . . . wine. It takes too long.

Sarah John loved us to eat together. We'd talk. Have some time. Alone . . . I came down here to find the sketches you did. Of Jenny.

Turner They're not in here.

Sarah Did you give them to her?

359

Turner No.

Sarah Do you love me?

Turner What?

Sarah I've been waiting. For you to love me. I thought it would happen. But it hasn't.

Turner What do you mean? . . . We don't argue.

Sarah I dreamt that you were with Jenny. That I was sat in the corner of our bedroom watching the two of you. And you were lying with your head next to her feet. And you were touching them very gently. And you were kissing her ankles. And you were just so happy.

Turner It was a dream. A fiction.

Sarah But I feel ashamed. Apologetic. And that's not me. If you want me gone you should tell me.

Turner I don't.

Sarah I need more, William.

Turner I don't know how to give more.

Sarah And I don't know how to live with this little.

Turner I'll try. To improve.

Sarah No. It's not school. When the baby's born. If you still want to. You can draw me. Nude.

Turner You don't want me to.

Sarah I've changed my mind.

Turner You don't have to do that.

Sarah I want to.

Turner No.

Sarah I want to. Please.

Turner Why?

Sarah I want you to draw me. I want you to.

Sarah kisses Turner's cheek and leaves him alone.

SCENE NINETEEN

The Academy. Turner lectures. William has pictures behind him. Turner and William both wear black mourning bands. William looks at the floor.

Turner Painting is a curiously private activity. Private. Then . . . public.

Silence.

You have to be strong enough. Agile. In your vision. To handle the public side of it. But then not to allow that to contaminate . . . your privacy. The independent artist. He will prefer to be a beggar and do good work than crawl to a patron and produce incompetent . . . scraps. An idea for a painting. 'A Burial at Sea.' Two tall fighting ships. And a tiny coffin between them. With the sun catching the coffin as it goes into the waves. The vastness of nature versus the small scale of man. In his box. Whilst live men are on two larger floating boxes. A painting is the most beautiful escape you could ever wish for.

Silence.

A picture.

Turner looks round. William has not reacted. Turner looks through the drawings. William looks at the students and at Turner. William sits down on the floor, puts his head in his hands. And weeps. Turner sees this. Then looks round at the students.

Laughing, are you? Laughing? I'll take you. Outside. Now.

He gathers himself.

Go back to your work. Go.

He looks at his students.

SCENE TWENTY

The studio. Turner sits opposite Jenny. She is pale.

Jenny Sorry.

Turner Don't keep apologising.

Jenny I just wanted to tell you. I'll go in a minute.

Turner Stay as long as you like. Dad can make a bed up for you.

Jenny No. Not many people knew him really. Apart from the other girls. And you.

Turner I wish you'd told me before.

Jenny Haven't been able to move. I just lay down for a week. Since I got up I've not really been thinking very straight.

Turner What can I do? To help?

Jenny Nothing. Everything's slower. Like I took opium. Wish I had.

Turner Are you in the same place?

Jenny I'll move. I can't stay there. Not now. It's full of him, you know?

Turner Can I do anything?

Jenny No one can. It's very strange. Like I can only think one thought at a time. It's like I've taken something. Thanks, though. Shall I come again?
    I need to do a few things. Or I'll just stop.

Turner Take some money.

Jenny No. I'd only get high on it. I might wake up and think he was still here.

Turner Please. Take it.

Jenny No. I don't need it for anything. He was beautiful, wasn't he?

Turner He was. And sharp. And his imagination –

Jenny He was kind too. If anyone was . . . he worried . . . about the children. He saw a family sleeping on the streets. He said we could put them in our bed with us. Do you have his drawings? I'd like them.

Turner has thrown them out.

Turner I'll look for them . . . after you've gone. The place is a mess.

Jenny You haven't got them, have you?

Turner Somewhere. Just . . . you know what it's like in here.

Jenny Don't worry. It's only bits of paper. It's not really him, is it?

Jenny cries. Turner cannot comfort her.

Will you walk me to the corner?

Turner takes a moment to reply.

Actually, don't.

She looks at Turner's model ships which are on a shelf in a glass casement.

He was crazy about those ships. He asked you for them, didn't he? You said they weren't a toy.

Turner I'm sorry.

Jenny No. You're right. They're not. But I don't think he wanted to play with them. He just wanted to put them in his corner. And look at them. Goodnight.

Jenny shakes his hand. And leaves.

SCENE TWENTY-ONE

The Academy. Turner lectures.

Turner We must aim as high in painting as the most exalted poets. Investigate the universal truths of our existence. 'And I saw an angel standing in the sun . . . and he cried with a loud voice . . . saying to all the fowls that fly in the midst of heaven, "Come and gather yourselves together unto the supper of the great God; that ye may eat the flesh of kings, and the flesh of captains and the flesh of mighty men, and the flesh of horses, and of them that sit on them, both small and great."'
Bathe in the past. Then forget it. Explode it.

Turner has slightly wandered. He comes back to his students.

Hannibal. He was told it was impossible to cross the Alps. Impossible. But he didn't listen . . . Rather like you, sir. Not listening.

Turner walks away.

SCENE TWENTY-TWO

The studio. Sarah sits and Turner checks a book for a quote. Sarah knits, heavily pregnant.

Sarah She's kicking.
What are you reading?

Turner Pope.

Sarah We could go to the Vauxhall Gardens tomorrow. If it's nice.

Turner I need a few hours in the morning.

Sarah We could luncheon there.

Turner Dad'll be doing his Sunday roast.

Sarah Yes.

Turner We could walk. Along the river.

Sarah Will you take your sketchbook?

Turner I thought I might.

*Sarah nods, resigned to it. Turner reads his book.
Sarah watches him, studies him.*

Sarah I'll enjoy the drawings you'll do of me. It will give me time to think.
I dreamt about the theatre last night. There was a man in the wings. And I couldn't see his face. But I could hear his breathing. And then he touched me. He stood behind me. And held me. And I didn't know if it was beautiful or frightening. We sort of became one body. And his breath was all over me. And running through me. And I didn't know whether to stay or go. He was taking me. And I came. In the dream. Very quietly. But violently.

Turner Was he me?

Sarah No.

Turner John?

Sarah No. He was someone else.

Turner kisses Sarah's brow. He puts his hand over her stomach so that he can feel the baby kicking. Sarah

puts her hand on his then takes his hand away. Gives
him his hand back.

SCENE TWENTY-THREE

The studio. Turner wears a mourning band. He paints.
We watch him, alone for a while. He is full of the
painting, but also of his father, who has died. He
lectures, but to no one.

Turner It's Hannibal. And he's crossing the Alps. There's
sky. And the sun. The men try to . . . shield themselves.
But up against them there is a vast dark cloud. It's about
to crash down. And there's snow. And storm. But
beyond that is a different sky. Beyond. It's white. The
sun is God and it's a battle. Of dark against light. God
versus inertia. Versus degradation. Versus pain. Versus
constraint. Versus lies. And all the . . . Versus
convention. Versus fear. And . . . the light has to win. It
does. Win. And it's beautiful. And violent. It's sublime.

'Dido's Lament' plays as Turner stares at us.
Behind him the vision of 'Hannibal Crossing the
Alps' appears.

Blackout.